Using Your Network

Making New Home Sales With People You Already Know

Using Your Network

Making New Home Sales With People You Already Know

Steve Hoffacker

CAPS, MCSP, MIRM

Using Your Network

Making New Home Sales With People You Already Know

Cover photo by Steve Hoffacker.

ALL RIGHTS RESERVED.

ISBN: 978-0-9843524-9-4

———

To sell new homes, you can wait for interested people to come to you from various sources of marketing and promotion, or you can go out and attract potential customers yourself. You can take responsibility for producing your own leads by intentionally meeting new people and developing those contacts — or you can generate new business by working with people that you already know and who know you.

———

Other New Home Sales Books By Steve Hoffacker

To find additional books on new home sales written by Steve Hoffacker, visit http://stevehoffacker.com/new homesalesbooks.html.

Titles are available in print (softbound) and as Kindle eBooks, and they include:

"Making The Grade: *The A-B-C's Of Rating New Home Customers*"

"Selling With Builders: *How Realtors® Can Profit From Selling Builders' New Homes*"

"Operation Discovery: *Who, What, When, Where, & More In New Home Sales*"

"Making New Friends: *Connecting With Strangers To Make More New Home Sales*"

"Universal Design For Builders: *Building & Selling Accessible, Safe & Comfortable New Homes*"

"Creating A Great First Impression: *Being An Effective New Home Sales Center Receptionist*"

"Fueling Your New Home Sales Business: *Making Strategic Contacts For More Sales & Referrals*"

Table Of Contents

Preface

I appreciate that you bought this book and that you are reading it — particularly because of the importance of this subject.

It demonstrates that you are interested in being an even better, stronger, more productive new home salesperson than you are right now.

It also shows me that you are willing to take personal responsibility for generating the leads that it will take to sustain you in business.

Market conditions vary, with traffic in some being slower and the number of sales less than what has been the case typically — for both new and existing homes.

Even in more stable market conditions, you might find that you want more traffic than you normally are getting through conventional or traditional means (print advertising, signage, brokers, and your website).

Still, regardless of what type of market conditions you may find yourself in, you can take responsibility for the amount of traffic that you get to work with.

You can impact the amount of business you have.

You literally can take matters into your own hands.

I like to think of the general theme of what I am presenting to you as "generating customers without advertising."

Typically, new homes are sold by having the customer (the interested party) visit your model home or new home sales center.

Usually they hear about your model home or new home community through advertising, such as the newspaper or your website. They may also see or notice a billboard or directional sign.

Nevertheless, these are ways of attracting customers to your location that your builder provides for you, and they can only do so much to bring new customers to your sales center.

Sometimes this is sufficient to make the number of sales that you or your company want you to make. Sometimes it isn't.

Even in good markets, you can supplement the amount of traffic you are receiving and the number of sales you are making by using the concepts and techniques in this book.

However, when sales are slow or you are competing with other builders or colleagues for a finite number of new home customers, the techniques in this book can make all the difference in how successful you are.

I want you to be a self-generator of traffic.

I don't want you to feel like you have to rely solely on traffic that walks through your front door that you had no hand in generating.

I don't want you to be dependent just on the traffic that traditional or conventional types of advertising and promotion create for you.

In fact, I want you to act as though the only traffic that you get to work with is that produced from your own efforts.

Treat the traffic that your builder produces for you as a bonus.

If you work with other salespeople, this is traffic that you don't have to share or worry about losing to any other salesperson — because you will have identified and produced it yourself.

I realize that this is probably a major paradigm shift for you, but I want you to act as your entire income is going to come from the people that you produce through your own efforts.

Instead of wondering why you don't have more traffic or asking your builder to spend more money and run more ads, you now can do something about it. You can be in control.

You can do this with no direct cost to your builder other than your typical telephone, email, and postage usage.

This text provides strategies and techniques for generating many potential customers for you and your company by working with people you already know or those that are referred to you.

There are specific telephone and in-person scenarios as well as email and letter templates that you can use exactly as they are (or close to it), or you can use them as a guide to develop your own style of contact.

It's time to take an active role in generating more traffic and sales, and this text is specifically geared toward helping you develop leads from people that you already know — your existing circle of contacts.

Using Your Network

Making New Home Sales With People You Already Know

1

Why Generate Your Own Leads?

Typical Advertising Is Builder-Driven

If you're like most new home salespeople, you don't get to control or influence how most of your customers learn about your homes or contact you.

While many people will tell you that they were driving by when they stopped into your sales center (because that's the easiest response and doesn't require any elaboration), most of your traffic probably visits you because they saw some type of print ad in a newspaper or magazine (such as a real estate publication or new homes guide), noticed a directional sign (bootleg, bandit, or snipe sign) or billboard, or visited your website.

Perhaps you have radio or television advertising.

Brokers may bring interested people as well, and people who have seen your new homes or actually purchased one may tell their friends and relatives about you.

Nevertheless, most customers typically visit your model home or new home sales center through the efforts (and investment) of your builder or your company.

Essentially, under this arrangement, there is little direct impact that you can have.

Typical Advertising Is Passive

Regardless of what type of advertising is the most successful for you and your company — or what type you personally favor — the fact is that typical advertising, marketing, and promotion is *passive*.

There is nothing wrong or bad about this except that you can't count it — specifically.

You can run ads, broadcast radio and TV spots, send out direct mail, post signs and billboards — and it's all passive. The person who has a need for what you're offering has to see the message, identify with it, and then act upon it. That's what makes it passive.

There's no way to know how many people or which specific people are going to respond to your message until your front door opens, your telephone rings, or you get an email request for information.

Changing The Formula

The issue with builder-supplied (passive) traffic is that it's not always as plentiful or consistent as you might like.

The main drawback is that you are not in control.

There's nothing wrong with builder-generated traffic. In fact, it's an important source of your leads.

Nevertheless, if you did nothing more than just work with the traffic that was generated through conventional builder-driven advertising and promotion, you would not be able to impact your traffic numbers at all.

You would just have to settle for who showed up and when they arrived.

However, you can be more in control of the amount — and quality — of the traffic that you receive and get to work with than you are when you just rely on builder-generated traffic.

Suppose newspaper advertising, website visits, or other conventional ways of producing traffic aren't enough for you.

What if real estate agents aren't bringing enough people for you to work with on a consistent basis?

How can you make more traffic materialize?

The answer is by going after it and creating it. Take responsibility for it.

Starting With People Closest To You

Without thinking about it too hard — or getting out a pad and pencil to begin writing down names — there are many people you already know that can begin helping you to grow your business.

The reason most of them haven't so far is because you haven't asked for their help.

You may have relatives living near you, and everyone has neighbors — as well as a circle of contacts, friends and other acquaintances.

Depending on where you went to school and how long ago that was, you might also have several former classmates and alumni friends that you see on a regular basis or ones that you maintain contact with.

The key in generating leads is tapping into this network of people that you already know to make sure they know what you're doing and that you can use their help.

People Enjoy Helping Each Other

People like to help you when they can. This is a characteristic that all of us have within us.

People enjoy helping each other if they feel that they can and as long as they aren't seriously inconvenienced by doing so.

However, not everyone may be willing or able to help you. That's all right.

Start with the people you know the best and then go from there.

What you are looking for are some people that you already know (even ones that you don't know that well or you haven't spoken to in a while) who might have an interest themselves in the homes you are offering — or who at least will be able to lead you to other people that they know.

The contacts — through suggestions and introductions — that your friends, relatives, and acquaintances provide for you will include people that you have not met or hadn't thought of who might have an interest in your homes.

The key to this concept is reaching out to people you already know to let them help you.

There is power in reaching out to people that you already know and in requesting their help to generate new leads.

They want to help, and you certainly can use their help. It's a win-win.

Focusing On People You Know

There are two basic ways to reach out to others for their help in generating leads for your business. One is reaching out to strangers, and I discuss these strategies in a companion book, *"Making New Friends — Connecting With Strangers To Make More New Home Sales."*

The other is working with people you already know. That is the subject of this book.

For the examples and strategies that I present in this book, I'm talking about people that you know well or at least have spoken to before and would recognize your name or take your call.

You may decide to call upon family, current or former neighbors, business associates, professional contacts, merchants that you patronize, service providers and suppliers that you use, former classmates from high school or college or real estate school, brokers and other real estate agents, appraisers, home inspectors, home stagers, lenders, mortgage brokers, sorority or fraternity members, military buddies, social acquaintances, members from the church or civic groups that you belong to, people who have purchased homes from you, friends of your spouse or children that you've met, people to whom you have made a presentation who are not interested in what you have to offer, or anyone else that you have met in the past.

Time Of Friendship Doesn't Matter

The length of time that you have known someone is not important.

The period of time that has passed since you last spoke with them or saw them in person is not important either.

The fact that you can call someone by name — because you know them and they know you — is more important than how long you've known them, how well you know them, or long it's been since your last contact with them.

You might be life-long friends with someone, or you may only know someone that you only met briefly at a social function, seminar, or gathering.

Whether you talk to someone frequently or it was just that one time when you introduced yourselves to each other, people still enjoy helping other people.

People will even help total strangers change a tire, give directions, make up small change at the checkout, phone for assistance, or carry their packages.

If we are willing to do that for people that we don't even know because they need our help and we can supply it, think of how much more people we already know might be willing to help us.

As long as your request seems reasonable to them, people will generally endeavor to help you if they feel they can.

You're Not Risking Your Friendship

Don't worry about imposing on your friendship or making people uneasy that you've approached them.

You're not going to be asking people to go out-of-their way or go the extra-mile to help you.

You just want to know if they know anyone — including themselves — who are looking for a new home that might be interested in what you are building.

You're not trying to use your friendship with someone to undermine or exploit it.

You simply want to tap into their circle of contacts to expand the number of people you can talk to about your opportunity.

As long as you do nothing to jeopardize your relationship, you should not be concerned about the simple act of asking people you already know for their help.

You May Not Get Any Help Right Now

The people you talk to may not be able to think of anyone to recommend to you, or the one or two people that they do recall may be looking for something different than what you offer.

Still, your friends will have tried to help you.

This is not necessarily a one-time request either.

Someone that you approach now may not be able to think of anyone to refer to you at that moment — or what you are selling currently doesn't match their needs of those of their friends, but they might be able to recommend someone the next time you talk with them or for homes you build in the future.

They might even bring it up later on their own as they think of someone.

Raising Their Awareness

If you sincerely believe that you represent a good product at a reasonable value that will meet the needs of anyone who is looking for what you are offering, you shouldn't hesitate about sharing your story with as many people as possible.

This is why you start with people that you know.

You want to help them, and you can use their help.

Approach your friends, relatives, clients, associates, acquaintances, past customers, and others in your circle of contacts.

If nothing more, you are raising their consciousness and awareness so now they are beginning to think of ways to help you.

It's a fairly reasonable request.

You simply are approaching people that you already know and asking for their help — and it's human nature for people to want to try to help if they can.

Whether you are calling someone, emailing them, sending them a letter or card, or seeing them in-person, you simply are asking people if they can help you meet someone that you can talk to about your new homes.

There's No Obligation

If one of your friends doesn't want to help you or isn't able to provide any names for you, that's all right.

Your friendship or relationship doesn't depend on them being able to help you with a referral.

Just keep trying until you get some help.

You're not trying to create any feeling of guilt or obligation — where they feel they have to look at your homes or give you some names or else you will be disappointed in them.

If people that you already know don't have an interest in your product, that's OK. Maybe they'll be able to lead you to someone else who might be.

And on it goes — there's tremendous potential.

The more people you involve in helping you search for potential customers, the more successful you will be at identifying them.

Working For Yourself

Be thankful for the traffic that your builder (through the advertising, signage, direct mail, internet, and other sources) generates for you, but be confident in your own abilities to go beyond that and produce your own leads.

If you work in a sales center with other people, you won't have to worry about sharing the leads that you generate for yourself.

You will have produced them, and you can work with them.

Allowing other people that you already know to help you locate and identify people to talk with about your new homes is a great way to supplement the traffic that you get through traditional advertising, signage, and the internet.

You may even get to the point where you will be responsible for the majority of the leads that you get.

In fact, a great attitude or paradigm is to regard all of the traffic generated by your company as a bonus and to plan on producing all of your own leads yourself.

2

Being A Traffic Generator

Going Past Regular Advertising

I trust that you are not content just to wait for a new customer to find you through the internet, newspaper ads, direct mail, new home guides, directional signage, or their real estate professional.

There's nothing wrong with this and it has been the mainstay of traffic production over the years, but it's just not dependable — and it's not sufficient.

While the majority of your business currently may come from these sources, it is not a long-term strategy for success because your competition has essentially the same access to these resources.

You need to be different — in a strategic way.

It takes initiative and innovation to be successful with lead generation.

Go beyond what your competitors are willing to do and take responsibility for producing your own traffic.

How often are there slack periods or lulls in the traffic when you wish that more traffic was coming in, that it was coming in more consistently, or that you could do something about making the telephone ring more often?

How about having your inbox fill up with qualified email inquiries, or the front door open more often with people qualified and interested in purchasing a new home such as you offer?

Don't Just Accept What You Get

You don't have to accept just what comes your way through conventional sources — from ads (print or web), signage, your website, brokers, or promotions.

You don't have to work just with the traffic that your builder provides. You can have considerably more than that and be instrumental in producing it.

You can be a catalyst in generating traffic and filling those void spots when traffic produced through other, more traditional sources is not as strong or consistent as you would like.

Taking Responsibility For More Traffic

Take it upon yourself to go outside the boundaries of your sales center to meet and talk to people you already know who might have a need for a new home such as you offer — or can lead you to other people that you can serve.

This is proactive, intentional contact, and it so often is the missing ingredient in being a totally productive new home salesperson.

These are advanced lead generation techniques, but anyone can use them.

In the pages of this book that you are now reading are powerful strategies and scenarios for increasing your customer base — all through reaching out to people you already know.

Not everyone who should know about your homes may find out about you through traditional means.

However, when you actively take your message outside the office, you can identify and approach additional people.

Rather than relying on the traffic that is produced though the efforts of your builder, you now can have a very real stake in the amount of people who visit you.

In fact, I have known salespeople who have created such a broker following and referral base that they actually have decided not to take any walk-in or non-"ask-for" traffic.

Of course, if you are in a one-person office, this wouldn't be such a concern — except that you will have created additional traffic for yourself.

The point is, however, that you can create and produce a substantial portion of your traffic — even as much as all of it — through referrals and proactive self-generation of leads.

Not A Mandatory Action

No one is forcing you to produce your own sales leads, but I imagine that this is important to you since you are reading this book.

Just think of the advantage that you'll have over other new home salespeople in your marketplace when you become responsible for producing your own leads rather than just relying on customers produced through conventional forms of marketing and traffic generation.

Think of the difference you can make in the advertising budget of your company by being a responsible, effective producer of traffic and sales without using conventional resources.

Is Self-Generation For You?

Before you get started on your program of generating your own leads to supplement or even replace the traffic that your builder provides for you now, it's important to make the commitment to yourself that this is something that you want to do.

Don't undertake it lightly. It is going to require time, effort, dedication, and persistence to conduct it properly.

If you already are making so many presentations that you really couldn't comfortably meet another customer during your workday, you may not need to generate any more customers on your own — especially if your sales output is at an acceptable level.

However, conditions are subject to change, and in the future you may find that your traffic is less abundant.

If traffic is slower than you anticipated or less than you would like to have through builder-driven advertising or lead production, you can become a traffic generator to make up for the shortfall.

This is especially true if you are the type of person who likes to have even more traffic than you already have.

Then definitely you should become a traffic generator.

Traffic Generation Is Empowering

Knowing that you have the ability to generate your own traffic to supplement what you get — or fail to get — through more traditional means should be very empowering to you.

It can propel you into success while others in your marketplace are struggling or working with the traffic that they customarily get.

Being a traffic-generator means that you never have to be totally dependent upon your company's advertising or marketing for bringing in enough traffic for you to be successful.

It means that people that you already know — or their friends and relatives that you can meet — may show up in your sales center for a presentation.

This creates a predisposition for liking your homes before you ever begin your presentation, and they are going to like you and enjoy what you have to say because they are friends of yours — or friends of friends. This is true even if they decide not to purchase.

You have the power to generate your own leads, and this will shape the future of your business.

3

Getting Started

Making The Commitment

The first step in creating additional traffic for yourself is actually making the commitment to begin doing something about the amount and quality of leads that you get.

It's strictly a voluntary program. However, it's willful, intentional, and proactive. It's up to you — and only you — to implement and execute.

It's making the definite decision that you want to go beyond what is produced for you through traditional or conventional advertising, promotions, signage, web pages, brokers, and casual referrals (those people that will come in because a friend told them about you).

Once you make the commitment, you can go about accomplishing it. You can formulate a plan. You can have a strategy.

You have so many resources available to you, and working with people you already know is a great way to build your customer base.

Beginning At The Beginning

The easiest and quickest place to start building leads for yourself is with people you already know — regardless of how well you know them or for how long.

It doesn't even matter how long it's been since you last talked with them.

Begin with the most obvious ones: family, friends and acquaintances, local brokers, and existing homeowners that you've already made sales to or ones you've met who were already living in your neighborhood when you started with your company.

Then you can progress to local professionals, businesses, and people you frequent for goods and services, and friends of friends.

Don't forget to involve your business contacts and acquaintances from church, chambers of commerce, builder or real estate associations, organizations like Rotary clubs, or other business or civic organizations where you might be a member.

Think beyond the obvious.

Spreading The Word

Don't make any assumptions about your relatives, friends, and acquaintances knowing what you do.

Have you told all of them what you're doing?

Do they realize that you sell real estate? New homes?

Are they aware of the opportunities that you have?

Are you sure?

Are they willing to lead you to others?

It's time to find out what they know and how willing they are to help you.

Who Do They Know?

When you begin reaching out to your friends, relatives, acquaintances, and circle of contacts with a phone call, email, or personal visit, you are not contacting them to try to get them to purchase a new home with you — unless you've heard or they've already mentioned that they are in the market for a new home, or it comes out in the conversation.

You're looking past that. You want to plant the seeds and make sure they are aware of how they can help you.

The reason you contact them — and nearly everyone else that you contact proactively — is twofold: to make sure they know what you are doing so they can keep that in mind and to learn about and meet the people that they know.

Then you can contact those people to learn who is interested in your homes.

It is not necessary that you know someone well in order to begin a conversation with them about what you do and what you are offering.

Of course, selling new homes is your ultimate goal, but you must have people to talk with about your homes first.

This is the reason for self-generation of leads, and the reason you begin with your friends.

Just Making The Contact

When you talk with your friends or acquaintances — or the people they introduce you to — you are not trying to make a presentation or asking anyone to acquire a new home from you when you initially approach or contact them.

That is likely your ultimate goal, but initially you just need them to indicate a willingness to help you and then to express an interest in what you are offering, agree to take a look at your homes, or refer someone else to you.

All you are concerned about is making people aware of what you're doing and the opportunity you represent so that you can create some initial interest and possibly attract people to look at your homes — people that you know well enough to contact but who may not know what you're doing currently.

Remember that proactive, intentional contact here means just an introduction to what you're offering.

You're contacting people you already know or people that are referred to you by people that you know.

Therefore, this is not a cold call, and you don't need to establish yourself as someone they should talk to.

Whether it's a close friend that you just haven't discussed real estate with yet, someone that you haven't spoken with in a long time, or someone you just met briefly at a social event or business function, your proactive contact is meant to let them know what you're doing now and to let them know that you would like their help.

Ways To Make The Contacts

In this book, I provide formats, scripts, and scenarios to use in approaching or re-establishing contact with people you already know — through in-person face-to-face meetings, telephone conversations, and written contact.

You can use them as they are word-for-word, or you can adapt them to your own personal style.

The opportunities for proactive, intentional contact and renewing of acquaintances are extensive.

Think creatively for places and opportunities to contact or reconnect with people that you know and take your message to them.

As I have stressed, look beyond the obvious.

Sometimes you'll want to send an old friend an email or note. Possibly a holiday greeting card. Maybe a text message would even work.

Other times you might just want to drop in on someone or invite them to coffee or lunch.

Phone calls are quite versatile and work well when there's a good chance of actually connecting with the people you are trying to call rather than getting their voice mail or going through a receptionist or an assistant. Cellphones are a good place to start rather than the office phone because this is a more personal form of contact.

The point is, there are many ways to contact your family, friends, and acquaintances, and you can intersperse the methods and mix them up.

However, I would only use texting or instant messaging to set up a time to talk, for an appointment for coffee, or as a reminder or follow-up to an earlier conversation.

Your goal is more than just spreading your message. You also want to interact and get some help.

Working Just With People You Know

There are many opportunities for you to meet, contact, and reach out to people that you don't already know or have a relationship with — those you are approaching or meeting for the first time.

I discuss those scenarios and the many opportunities for your success in developing those relationships in my companion book *"Making New Friends — Connecting With Strangers To Make More New Home Sales."*

However, here I am strictly talking about contacting and working with people that you already know or have at least met briefly at a business or social event — anyone that you know well enough to pick up the phone and call and have them recognize your name and take your call.

Begin with your family and closest circle of friends.

It's important that you let them know what you are doing and that you would like to have their help in identifying potential purchasers for your product.

After all, you would do the same for them if they asked and you knew of some way to help them or someone to refer to them.

People Want To Help You

Whether this is a close family member, a distant relative, someone from the club or organization you belong to, someone from your former or current neighborhood, someone you went to school with, a friend or co-worker of your spouse, someone from activities or sports that you do with your kids, someone whose store you shop at, someone you met only long enough to exchange business cards, or anyone else that you know, the point is that you know — or at least have met — each other.

More than that, you know each other well enough for you to walk into their office, pick up the phone and call them, or send them a note or email and have them talk with you.

You know them well enough to be able to ask for their help and not feel awkward about the request.

Remember that people like to help other people when they can — especially people they know.

Don't feel that you need to know someone for a certain period of time before you talk with them about your business — or that people will think less of you because you want to talk business rather than engage in small talk.

Expanding Your Network

To begin generating your own leads, you just need to tell your story to more people than typically walk through your front door or contact you through traditional ways.

That's why your network of friends, relatives, neighbors, acquaintances, shop owners and managers, professionals whose services you use, friends of friends, and anyone else that you know become important — as you ask them for assistance in helping you identify potentially interested people that you haven't met. This will expand your network of people that you know.

Just be careful that you don't expect your proactive contact of people you already know to do more than it is designed to do.

The contact is not designed to make a sale. You won't be making a presentation or asking for an order.

You just want to identify people in your network to approach and discuss how you can use their help. Then you want to meet others that they know.

This will get you started generating your own traffic and free you from total reliance on the traffic that your builder provides.

It diminishes the reliance on passive marketing and puts you in control.

Four Possible Outcomes

Whether you are meeting and talking with strangers (not the subject of this book but a very important part of your overall lead generation strategy) or interacting with people that you already know, not everyone will have an immediate need for your services.

Some might eventually, but that's only part of the total picture.

When you approach your friends and people you already know and ask for their help, there are four possible outcomes — four things that can result.

First, they can refuse to help you. Don't let this stop you from talking with them. It's a possibility, but only one of four.

Maybe they think they can't help you or they don't want to get involved. Maybe they just don't want to help even though they know you. That's unfortunate, but shake it off and move on.

Second, they can have an immediate need to move out of their current home and get another one that they will tell you about, and you can engage and work directly with them.

This means that some of your friends and acquaintances become your customers themselves.

Third, they may not have an immediate need to start looking for a new home, but they will want one in the future — and they will share this information with you.

So, you have some friends and acquaintances who will become your future customers.

Fourth, they can introduce you or lead you to other people that they know whom they feel might have an interest in talking and working with you — with either an immediate or future need.

This is the power of reaching out to get help from the network of people you know.

Time To Get Started

Now, with all of this background on how you want to work with your friends, relatives, acquaintances, and others that you know to help you generate new leads that you can talk with about your homes, it's time to actually get started.

That begins on the next page where I present three consecutive chapters of scenarios for you to use in contacting people in-person, by telephone, and in writing (including electronic).

You won't use every approach with each person. Some you may only visit in person. Some you may only call. Some you will more than one approach.

Nevertheless, use these techniques as a starting point and add ones of your own that you like. Feel free to use your own words and style, but this will get you started.

4

Generating Leads In-Person

Opportunities To Interact With People

There are people around you constantly.

You shop, bike, jog, work-out at the club, run errands, pick up the kids or attend events with them (if you have kids), buy gas, eat lunch, get a coffee, go to the grocery store, get your car serviced, go to the doctor or dentist, talk with your attorney, drop off and pick up your clothes at the cleaners, live in your neighborhood, get your mail and packages, worship, eat dinner out, go places on your day off, go places with your spouse (if you're married), play golf, and go to the pool or beach.

You likely do even more than this in a week's time — considerably more. The point is that people are around you all the time.

It's learning to take advantage of these opportunities when you're around others to develop relationships and get their help in growing your business through the obvious networking possibilities that exist.

In some of your travels, you're going to see people that you already know or who are familiar to you by sight — even if you've never exchanged more than a glance, smile, wave, or "hello."

Sometimes you'll see complete strangers. You may or may not even have eye contact with them.

While this chapter focuses on connecting with people you already know or are familiar with, you will be making introductions to total strangers as well.

These former strangers then become people that you have at least met once — no matter how briefly — and then you can employ some of the contact strategies that I talk about in this book.

Making The Connection

In the next two chapters, I discuss ways for you to use telephone and written communication to reach out, contact, and connect with your network of people you already know and raise their awareness level so they will be in a position to work with you or refer others to you from their circle of contacts.

However, before we get to that, this chapter provides ways just to develop an in-person conversation to generate additional leads for yourself.

Use the scenarios (or ones like them) that I present in this chapter and the next two as a guide to developing relationships and referrals.

The suggested scripts in this chapter will help you as you contact people that you do business with, people you have met socially or at business functions, people that you see occasionally, family members, friends that you see often or rarely, people you have sold homes to or talked with during a presentation, or others that you will have an opportunity to talk with face-to-face about what you are doing and how you can use their help.

Adapting To Your Own Style

You'll discover from reviewing the scenarios and scripts that follow that there are many ways of saying the same thing — depending on your personal style and the degree of formality that might be called for at the time.

You can say *"I wanted to make sure you knew,"* or *"I'm not sure you are aware"* — or you can express a similar meaning by saying that *"I'm not sure if I ever mentioned,"* *"I don't know if I ever mentioned,"* *"In case I never mentioned,"* *"In case you didn't know,"* or *"I don't think I ever told you."*

Of course, you'll know the gender of your friends, but I have used the pronouns *"he," "his"* or *"him"* for convenience and to avoid using *"he/she/they"* or *"his/her/their"* or *"him/her/them."* Obviously, you would use the correct pronouns for the actual situation.

The same is true for people that you would like to have referred to you. They might be a single person or a couple, married or not. In many cases, I have just used the collective pronouns *"they," "their,"* or *"them."*

In actual usage, substitute the correct pronouns for the situation.

Visit To Businesses You Patronize

Use this scenario to talk with the owner, manager, proprietor, clerk, or employee you see frequently at a business you visit regularly. Even if you haven't talked much to this person other than exchanging smiles or nods, a friendly "hello," or some small talk, you know each other from your regular association. This would apply to such establishments as a bakery, donut or bagel shop, coffee shop, fast food restaurant, food catering trucks, hotel, gas station, convenience store, home improvement or décor center, gift shop, florist, furniture and accessories store, pharmacy, grocery, entertainment center, arcade, auto dealership, tire shop, boutique, equipment rental, hair salon, quick printer, car wash, bicycle shop, fitness center, auto detailer, post office or postal service store, marina, dry cleaner, tailor, or other businesses in your market that you visit on a regular basis. You want to make sure they are aware of what you do, discuss how they can help you, determine who they know that has an interest in buying a new home — and you'd like to display your business cards or flyers for their patrons.

———

"Hi <use their first name>."

[When you greet them, conduct your regular business, normal interaction, and small talk first. Then begin the following discussion about how you'd like their help.]

"Do you have a minute (Am I interrupting anything, Is this a convenient time)?"

NOW IS NOT A GOOD TIME — [You actually speak to your friend, owner, manager, or proprietor, but they are unable to devote any additional time to you now.] *"I'm sorry I caught you at an inconvenient (busy) time."*

"Have I ever mentioned to you (Do you remember that I said, I'm not sure I ever mentioned) that I represent <name of your company or community — or both> at <provide the actual location, address, or general description of the area — whatever would make the most sense to your friend>?"

"Well, I'd like your help on something."

"I'll stop back by when you have a couple of minutes (when you have time to talk). When would it be convenient for me to come back?"

[Don't get into a discussion now of what you're looking for — it will keep until your next visit.]

[Wait for response. Agree on a day and time for the return visit if other than your next regular visit to their establishment.]

"Would you like for me to come here, or would you let me buy you a cup of coffee?" [Wait for response about location of meeting — their business or store, or a coffee shop they suggest. Then confirm the location, day, and time.]

"Great. I'll see you <specify the day> at <location>. Thanks."

Is Available Now — [The person you want to speak to has time to talk now.] *"Great. I'll make this quick."*

"Have I ever mentioned to you (Do you remember that I said) that I represent <name of your company or community — or both> at <provide the actual location, address, or general description of the area - whatever would make the most sense to your friend>?"

"Well, I'd like your help."

"As you know, I've been trading (shopping, eating, drinking coffee) here for <approximate length of time such as a couple of years, 10 years, etc.>, and I thought maybe you could help me."

[Ask them if they have ever heard of your community or company, but it doesn't matter if they have.]

"We are building <state the number and/or type of homes, such as 18 custom homes, 62 single family homes, 212 homes in a golf course setting, affordable homes, entry-level homes, or luxury townhomes> from <state the price range of your homes>."

[Be careful not to share too much information about your opportunity. You are not trying to deliver a "mini-presentation" even though it might be tempting to do so. You just want to provide a basic description of what you offer so that you establish a frame of reference.]

"I thought that you might know of or possibly you might have heard of someone (two or three, three or four people) that might be in the market for a different home and that they should take a look at what we have to offer." [Wait for response — he or she might even say that they are personally interested.]

[If he or she volunteers a name or two, write it down and ask for a way to contact that person or persons. Be sure to note the correct spelling and pronunciation. Get first names so you don't sound like a telemarketer or solicitor when you call them, and get permission to use your friend's name when you contact the other people.]

They Have Names to Give You — *"That's great. I will call them and introduce myself and invite them to look at what we offer (what we have to offer) at <name of your community or company>."*

"I will call you after I have spoken with them to let you know what happened (how it went)."

"Can you think of anyone else?" [Wait for response.]

"Thanks for your help. See you next time. Good-bye."

No Names to Give You at This Time — *"That's quite all right."*

"I'd like to send you our newsletter on a periodic basis just so you will be aware of what we're offering."

"Is email OK, or should I just drop it off when I come in?" [Wait for the response. Confirm their email address or determine which one to use. You can also send them your contact information or vCard, and send them a link to your website and blog, if you have one.]

"Fine. If anyone does come to mind that you think should know about our community (homes), you can

either tell them about us directly or I would be happy to call them and invite them to take a look."

"In fact, let me give you some of my business cards so you'll have them available if you're talking to anyone that you think I should meet."

"If you can, let me know who was interested enough to take my card or who you gave one to."

"Would it be OK if I left some of my business cards on your counter or if I came back with a small display?" [Wait for response, and accept the answer either way.]

"You know, I'd love to show you what we have, and it might give you a better idea of what we're all about when you talk to people you know or think of who might be suited for what we offer."

"When I get back to the office, I'll check my calendar and give you a call to see when we're both available and schedule a time for you to visit. I'll buy the coffee." [Wait for the response. Either a "yes" or "no" is OK. It won't affect anything else you've discussed or the help you're looking for. It may not be convenient for him or her to visit now or they may feel that the appointment was what you wanted all along.]

"Thanks for your help. See you again next time. Good-bye."

Visit To Professionals You Patronize

Use this scenario to visit or talk with the owner, manager, principal, or partner of a professional services firm that you use on a regular basis — either personally or through your new home sales business. This would apply to such services as a doctor, dentist, attorney, tax preparer, accountant, ad agency, architect, consultant, appraiser, media people, webmaster, land planner, or others in your market that you or your company maintain a professional relationship with. You want to make sure they are aware of what you do, discuss how they can help you, determine who they know that has an interest in buying a new home — and you'd like to display your business cards or flyers for their patrons.

———

"Hi <use their first name>." [The person you are asking for might greet you, or there might be a receptionist. Ask for the person you came to see. If they aren't there or available, decide to wait if it will only be a few minutes, or politely say goodbye and return at another time. You don't need to set an appointment or leave any information. Make sure they know you're a friend or client.]

[When you greet them, give them your current business card, and conduct your regular business, normal interaction, and small talk first. Then begin the following discussion.]

"Do you have a minute (Is this a convenient time)?"

NOW IS NOT A GOOD TIME — [You actually speak to the person you are calling on, but they are unable to devote any additional time to you now.] *"I'm sorry I caught you at an inconvenient (busy) time. I realize that I just dropped in without an appointment."*

"I'll make this quick. Have I ever mentioned to you (Do you remember that I said) that I represent <name of your company or community — or both> at <provide the actual location, address, or general description of the area — whatever would make the most sense to them>?" [Wait for response, but it doesn't matter whether they remember or not.]

"Well, I'd like your help on something. I'll stop back by when you have a couple of minutes (when you have time to talk). When would it be convenient for me to come back?"

[Don't get into a discussion now of what you're looking for — it will keep until your next visit. Wait for response. Agree on a day and time for the return visit if other than your next regular visit to their establishment.]

"Would you like for me to come here, or would you let me buy you a cup of coffee?" [Wait for response about location of meeting — their business or store or a coffee shop they suggest. Then confirm the location, day, and time.] *Great. I'll see you <specify the day> at <location>. Thanks."*

IS AVAILABLE NOW — [The person you came to see has time to talk with you now.] *"Great. I'll make this quick."*

"Have I ever mentioned to you (Do you remember that I said) that I represent <name of your company or community — or both> at <provide the actual location, address, or general description of the area — whatever would make the most sense to your friend>?"

"Well, I'd like your help. I've been coming here (using your services) for <approximate length of time such as a couple of years, 10 years, etc.>, and I thought maybe you could help me."

[Ask them if they have ever heard of your community or company, but it doesn't matter if they have.]

"We are building <state the number and/or type of homes, such as 18 custom homes, 62 single family homes, 212 homes in a golf course setting, affordable homes, entry-level homes, or luxury townhomes> from <state the price range of your homes>."

[Be careful not to share too much information about your opportunity. You are not trying to deliver a "mini-presentation" even though it might be tempting to do so. You just want to provide a basic description of what you offer so that you establish a frame of reference.]

"This is where I need your help."

"I thought that you might know of, or possibly you might have heard of say a couple of (three or four) people that might be in the market for a different home and that they should take a look at what we have to offer." [Wait for response — he or she might even say that they are personally interested.]

[If he or she volunteers a name or two, write it down and ask for a way to contact that person or persons. Be sure to note the correct spelling and pronunciation. Get first names so you don't sound like a telemarketer or solicitor when you call them, and get permission to use your friend's name when you contact the other people.]

They Have Names to Give You — *"That's great. I will call them and invite them to look at what we offer at <name of your community or company>. Then, I will call you after I have spoken with them to let you know what happened."*

"Can you think of anyone else?" [Wait for response.]

"Thanks for your help. See you next time. Good-bye."

No Names to Give You at This Time — *"That's quite all right."*

"I'd like to send you our newsletter on a periodic basis just so you will be aware of what we're offering. Is email OK, or should I just drop it off when I come in?"

[Wait for the response. Confirm their email address or determine which one to use. You can also send them your contact information or vCard and send them a link to your website and blog, if you have one.]

"Fine. If anyone does come to mind that you think should know about our community (homes), you can either tell them about us directly, or I would be happy to call them and invite them to take a look."

"In fact, let me give you some of my business cards so you'll have them available if you're talking to anyone that you think I should meet."

"If you can, let me know who was interested enough to take my card or who you gave one to."

"Would it be OK if I left some of my business cards on your counter or if I came back with a small display?" [Wait for response, and accept the answer either way.]

"You know, I'd love to show you what we have, and it might give you a better idea of what we're all about when you talk to people you know or think of who might be suited for what we offer."

"When I get back to the office, I'll check my calendar and give you a call to see when we're both available and schedule a time for you to visit. I'll buy the coffee." [Wait for the response. Either a "yes" or "no" is OK. It

won't affect anything else you've discussed or the help you're looking for. It may not be convenient for him or her to visit now or they may feel that the appointment was what you wanted all along.]

"Thanks for your help. See you again next time. Good-bye."

Visit To Banks And Lenders

Use this scenario to talk to the manager, loan officer, or employee of a bank or lending institution that you use for your personal banking, where you have your home mortgage or other consumer loans, and/or where your builder has loans or a preferred lending relationship. You want to make sure they are aware of what you do, discuss how they can help you, determine who they know that has an interest in buying a new home — especially from people who have prequalified for a mortgage loan without a specific new home in mind. Also, you'd like to display your business cards or flyers for their patrons.

———

"Hi <use their first name>."

[If the person you came to see is not visible to you, ask for them. If they aren't there or available, you can choose to wait a few minutes or politely say goodbye and return at another time. You don't need to set an appointment or leave any information.]

[When you greet them, give them your current business card, and conduct your regular business, normal interaction, and small talk first. Then begin the following discussion.]

"Do you have a minute (Is this a convenient time)?"

NOW IS NOT A GOOD TIME — [You actually speak to the person you came to see, but they are unable to devote any additional time to you now.] *"I'm sorry I caught you at an inconvenient (busy) time. I know you're busy so I'll be very brief."*

"Have I ever mentioned to you (Do you remember that I said) that I represent <name of your company or community — or both> at <provide the actual location, address, or general description of the area — whatever would make the most sense to them>?" [It doesn't really matter how they answer this. Just continue.]

"Well, I'd like your help on something. I'll stop back by when you have a couple of minutes (when you have time to talk)."

"When would it be convenient for me to come back?" [Don't get into a discussion now of what you're looking for — it will keep until your next visit.]

[Wait for response. Agree on a day and time for the return visit if other than your next regular visit to their facility.]

"Would you like for me to come here, or would you let me buy you a cup of coffee?" [Wait for response about location of meeting — their business or a coffee shop they suggest. Then confirm the location, day, and time.]

"Great. I'll see you <specify the day> at <location>. Thanks."

Is AVAILABLE NOW — [The person you came to see has time to talk with you now.] *"Great. I'll make this quick."*

"Have I ever mentioned to you (Do you remember that I said) that I represent <name of your company or community — or both> at <provide the actual location, address, or general description of the area — whatever would make the most sense to your friend>?" [It doesn't really matter how they answer this. Just continue.]

"Well, I'd like your help."

[Ask them if they have ever heard of your community or company, but it doesn't matter if they have. If they are the lender for your company or community, obviously they will be familiar with your property and you won't need to ask this question. Just continue with your conversation.]

"We are building <state the number and/or type of homes, such as 18 custom homes, 62 single family homes, 212 homes in a golf course setting, affordable

homes, entry-level homes, or luxury townhomes> from *<state the price range of your homes>."* [If they know your property, just reiterate this.]

[Be careful not to share too much information about your opportunity. You are not trying to deliver a "mini-presentation" even though it might be tempting to do so. You just want to provide a basic description of what you offer so that you establish a frame of reference.]

"I thought that you might have talked to some people who came in to get pre-approved or pre-qualified for a mortgage loan before they actually located or settled on the home they want." [Wait for response.]

"I certainly would appreciate you telling them about me and what we offer so that I could show them our homes to see if there was any interest on their part."

[Wait for response and determine how he or she is going to notify those potential buyers or if they want you to do the contacting after they clear it with those people.]

"Also, I thought that outside of banking you might possibly know of or have heard of a couple of people that might be in the market for a different home and that they should take a look at what we have to offer."

[Wait for response — he or she might even say that they are personally interested.]

[If he or she volunteers a name or two, write it down and ask for a way to contact that person or persons. Be sure to note the correct spelling and pronunciation. Get first names so you don't sound like a telemarketer or solicitor when you call them, and get permission to use your friend's name when you contact the other people.]

They Have Names to Give You — *"That's great. I will call them and invite them to look at what we offer at <name of your community or company>. Then, I will call you after I have spoken with them to let you know what happened."*

"Can you think of anyone else?" [Wait for response.]

"Thanks for your help. See you next time. Good-bye."

No Names to Give You at This Time — *"That's quite all right. I'd like to send you our newsletter on a periodic basis just so you will be aware of what we're offering. Is email OK, or should I just drop it off when I come in?"*

[Wait for the response. Confirm their email address or determine which one to use. You can also send them your contact information or vCard and send them a link to your website and blog, if you have one.]

"If anyone does come to mind that you think should know about what we offer, you can either tell them about us directly or I would be happy to call them."

"In fact, let me give you some of my business cards so you'll have them available if you're talking to anyone that you think I should meet."

"If you can, let me know who was interested enough to take my card or who you gave one to."

"Would you have a place where I could leave some of my business cards or put out a small display?" [Wait for response, and accept the answer either way.]

"Thanks for your help. See you again next time. Good-bye."

"Working The Room" With People You Know At A Business Or Social Event

Use this scenario to talk with people you already know when you see them at a social event or business function. This can include parties, receptions, mixers, get-togethers, barbeques, seminars, classes, trade shows, potluck dinners, ice cream socials, homebuilder or broker functions or meetings, and similar meetings and events. After the small talk, seek their help in identifying people interested in your new homes. You are looking for them to provide an introduction for anyone in the room or event that they feel you should meet. Otherwise, this is a prelude to a longer conversation or meeting outside of the event.

_____

"Hi, <first name of your friend>."

[After you exchange greetings and catch up on what each other has been doing, trade business cards if you don't have current contact information for each other. Give yours out anyway. Talk briefly about your homes and what you offer. Then, change gears and use the conversation to talk about what you want.]

"I'm working with <name of your company or community — or both> — and we're located at <a general description is probably enough>."

"I could really use your help, and I thought maybe you could identify some people — possibly even some who are here — who might be interested in looking for a new home in my area —- now or in the near future. Possibly some people that you know that I don't."

"Anyone come to mind right now that you have seen here that you think I should meet?" [Wait for response.]

[If yes, ask your friend to introduce you to them. If not, go to the next question.] *"Who (Who else) can you think of that might take my call to let them know about our homes?"* [Wait for response.]

[If they volunteer a name or two, write it down and ask for a way to contact that person or persons. Be sure to note the correct spelling and pronunciation. Get first names so you don't sound like a telemarketer or solicitor when you call them, and get permission to use their name when you contact the other people.]

[If your company offers an incentive for referrals, discuss this inducement for providing names. If they don't have any names now but agree to help you, set up a time to call them to get their referrals.]

"By the way, let me give you some of my business cards so you'll have them available if you're talking to anyone that you think I should meet. And if you can, let me who you gave one to."

"Also, I'd like to send you our newsletter on a periodic basis just so you will be aware of what we're offering. Is email OK?" [Wait for the response.]

[Confirm their email address or determine which one to use. You can also email them your contact information or vCard and send them a link to your website and blog, if you have one.]

[Discuss your next contact and agree on when and where that is to be and if it's going to be by email, phone, or in-person. You might set a time to get together for breakfast or coffee depending on how close your offices are to each other.]

"I'll talk to (see) you again then. Really great talking to

you. Thanks for your help. Goodbye. "

An Unexpected Meeting With A Friend

Use this scenario to talk with a friend or acquaintance that you happen to see unexpectedly someplace in public — regardless of how well you know them or how long it's been since you've seen or talked with them. Use this unplanned and impromptu meeting to reestablish and renew your relationship. You want to make sure they know what you're doing now and mention to them that you can use their help in finding people interested in your new homes. You may not be able to accomplish all of this in a brief, chance encounter. A subsequent phone call, email, or another meeting might be required.

"Hi, <first name of friend that you meet in public>. "

[After you exchange greetings and catch up on what each other has been doing, trade business cards if the contact information has changed. Hand out yours anyway. This may be the extent of what you can accomplish during this brief meeting.]

[If your friend that you are meeting does not have a card, be prepared to write down his or her contact information or have them write it for you on the back of one of your business cards. If you have them write down the information for you, be sure to inspect what they have provided, make sure you can read all of it, and confirm it with them. You know their name, but their preferred phone number and email is what you really need to get.]

JUST A BRIEF CONVERSATION — *"I'd really like to learn more about what you are doing these days and have a chance to tell you about what we're doing. I possibly could use your help."*

"When would it be convenient for me to call you so we could talk some more?" [Wait for response and agree on a day and time for the call.]

"Great, I'll call you <day and time agreed on>."

"Nice seeing you again. Goodbye."

A LONGER CONVERSATION — *"I'd really like to learn more about your business and what you do."* [Let him or her talk, listen to what they say, and ask questions — pay particular attention to the types of people he or she might know or the clientele served to frame your question for referrals.]

"I could sure use your help. We are building <describe briefly your homes, the price range, and location> and I was wondering who you might know that is in the market for a different home that I might talk to?"

[If you have amenities, special features, special construction techniques, energy saving programs, or anything else that would help who you're talking to think of potential names for you, mention them.]

"Who comes to mind (Can you think of one or two people) that falls into this category? (Who is the first person who comes to mind when I ask this question?)" [Wait for a response.]

[If he or she readily volunteers a name or two, write it down and ask for a way to contact that person or persons. Be sure to note the correct spelling and pronunciation. Get first names so you don't sound like a telemarketer or solicitor, and get permission to use your friend's name when you contact the other people they are furnishing. If your company offers an incentive for referrals, discuss this inducement for providing names.]

They Have Names to Give You — *"That's great. I will call them and invite them to take a look at what we offer at <name of your community or company>. Then, I will call you after I have spoken with them to let you know what happened."*

"Can you think of anyone else?" [Wait for response.] *"Thanks for your help. Great seeing you again."*

"By the way, if you don't mind, let me give you some of my business cards so you'll have them available if you're

talking to anyone that you think I should meet. And if you can, let me who was interested enough to take my card or who you gave one to."

"Goodbye."

No Names to Give You at This Time — "That's quite all right."

"I'd like to keep in touch with you and send you our newsletter on a periodic basis just so you will be aware of what we're offering. Is email OK?" [Wait for the response. Confirm their email address or determine which one to use. You can also send them your contact information or vCard and send them a link to your website and blog, if you have one.]

"If anyone does come to mind that you think I should talk with about our community (homes), you can have them contact me directly, or you can let me know and I'll be happy to call and invite them to come and take a look at what we have."

"I will call you in a few weeks just to let you know how things are progressing at <name of your community or company> and make sure that you have received what I have sent."

"In fact, if you don't mind, let me give you some of my business cards so you'll have them available if you're *talking to anyone that you think I should meet. And if you can, let me know who was interested enough to take my card or who you gave one to.*"

"*You know, I'd love to show you what we have, and it might give you a better idea of what we're all about when you talk to people you know or think of who might be suited for what we offer.*"

"*When I get back to the office, I'll check my calendar and give you a call to see when we're both available and schedule a time for you to visit. I'll buy the coffee.*" [Wait for the response. Either a "yes" or "no" is OK. It won't affect anything else you've discussed or the help you're looking for. It may not be convenient for him or her to visit now or they may feel that the appointment was what you wanted all along.]

"*I really appreciate your help. Great seeing you again. Goodbye.*"

Chance Meeting With A Broker Friend

Use this scenario to talk with a broker that you know that you happen to see someplace in public — regardless of how well you know them, how long it's been since you've seen or talked with them, or if you've ever done business together. Use this impromptu meeting to renew your relationship. You want to make sure they know what you're doing now and mention that you can use their help in finding people interested in your new homes. You may not be able to accomplish all of this in a brief, chance encounter so a subsequent phone call, email, or meeting might be required.

———

"Hi, <first name of broker friend you meet in public>."

[Exchange greetings, learn what each other has been doing since you last talked, and trade business cards.]

[Your friend should have a business card, but if they don't, be prepared to write down their contact information on the back of one of your cards. If you have them write the information, be sure to check it, make sure you can read all of it, and confirm it with them.]

JUST A BRIEF CONVERSATION — *"I'd really like to hear more about how you're doing these days and have a chance to tell you about what we're doing. And I sure could use your help."*

"When would be a convenient (good) time for me to call you or for us to have coffee?" [Wait for response, determine which they prefer, and agree on the time, and location for the call or visit.]

"Great. I'll call you <day and time agreed on>."

"Nice seeing you again. Goodbye."

A Longer Conversation — *"I'd really like to hear more about your business and how you're doing these days. I'd also like to tell you a little bit about what we're doing."*

[Let him or her talk, listen to what they say, and ask questions about their business and their market experiences — pay particular attention to the types of people he or she might know or the clientele served to frame your question for referrals.]

[As succinctly as you can, explain what you are building, your location, price range, opportunity, USP, and how it's being received so far. Don't give a mini-presentation but share enough with them about what you are offering to establish a reference point and create a level of interest.]

"I'm trying to build my customer base and sure could use another sale this month. How about you?" [Wait for response.]

"Are you working with anyone (Who are you working with) that you could bring by to look at what we have to offer?" [Wait for response.]

Has a Customer for You — *"That's great. When would it be convenient (When would be a good time) for you to visit?"* [Allow your friend to set the time and day for the visit and then agree to it — unless they can't commit to a specific time or you aren't sure of your schedule. In that case, agree on a time for you to call them to set an appointment.]

"Great, I'll call (see) you <day and time agreed on>."

"Nice seeing you again. Goodbye."

No Customers for You at This Time — *"That's quite all right."*

"I'd like to send you our newsletter periodically just so you will be aware of what we're offering. Is email OK?" [Wait for the response. Confirm their email address or determine which one to use. You can also send them your contact information or vCard and send them a link to your website and blog, if you have one.]

"By the way, why don't you stop by so I can show you around and we can visit a little more at that time?"

Agrees to visit — *"Fine. When's (What's) a good time for you to visit?"* [Set a convenient day and time for you the visit.]

"Great, I look forward to showing you our homes and community. Would you like for me to call or email you a reminder?" [Wait for response.]

Yes — *"Fine. I'll send you a note on <mention the*

specific day> to remind you of our appointment on <mention the day and time>. Which email address should I use?" [Confirm the address or write it down as you obtain it.]

"See you then. Goodbye."

No — "Fine. I'll plan on seeing you then <day and time>. Goodbye."

Does not want to visit — "That's fine. If you do meet anyone that you think should know about our community (homes), you can either stop by with them or call for an appointment. Either way, I'll be happy to work with you."

"I'll call you in a few weeks just to let you know how things are progressing at <name of your community or company> and to see how you're doing."

"I really appreciate your help."

"Great seeing you again. Goodbye."

Visit With A Broker Friend

Use this scenario to talk with a broker friend of yours when you drop into their office to meet with them or visit them at an open house they are hosting. Use this to renew your relationship — especially if it's been a while since you've seen or talked with them. You want to make sure they know what you're doing now and mention that you can use their help in finding people interested in your new homes. You may not be able to accomplish all of this during an unscheduled visit, so a subsequent phone call, email, or meeting might be required.

———

"Hi, <first name of broker friend>."

[Exchange greetings, learn what each other has been doing since you last talked, and trade business cards.]

[Your friend should have a business card, but if they don't, be prepared to write down their contact information on the back of one of your cards. If you have them write the information, be sure to check it, make sure you can read all of it, and confirm it with them.]

JUST A BRIEF CONVERSATION — *"I'd really like to hear more about how you're doing these days and have a chance to tell you about what we're doing. And I sure could use your help."*

"When would be a convenient (good) time for us to have coffee (talk again)?" [Wait for response, determine which they prefer, and agree on the day, time, and location for the call or visit.] *"Great. I'll call (see) you <day and time agreed on>."*

"Nice seeing you again. Goodbye."

A LONGER CONVERSATION — *"I'd really like to hear more about your business and how you're doing these days. I'd also like to tell you a little bit about what we're doing."*

[Let him or her talk, listen to what they say, and ask questions about their business and their market experiences — pay particular attention to the types of people he or she might know or the clientele served to frame your question for referrals.]

[As succinctly as you can, explain what you are building, your location, price range, opportunity, USP, and how it's being received so far. Don't give a mini-presentation but share enough with them about what you are offering to establish a reference point and create a level of interest.]

"I'm trying to build my customer base and sure could use another sale this month. How about you?" [Wait for response.]

"Are you working with anyone (Who are you working with) that you could bring by to look at what we have to offer?" [Wait for response.]

Has a Customer for You — *"That's great. When would it be convenient (When would be a good time) for you to* *visit?"* [Allow your friend to set the time and day for the visit and then agree to it — unless they can't commit to a specific time or you aren't sure of your schedule. In that case, agree on a time for you to call them to set an appointment.]

"Great, I'll call (see) you <day and time agreed on>."

"Nice seeing you again. Goodbye."

No Customers for You at This Time — *"That's quite all right."*

"I'd like to send you our newsletter periodically just so you will be aware of what we're offering. Is email OK?" [Wait for the response. Confirm their email address or determine which one to use. You can also send them your contact information or vCard and send them a link to your website and blog, if you have one.]

"By the way, why don't you stop by so I can show you around and we can visit a little more at that time?"

> **Agrees to visit** — *"Fine. When's (What's) a good time for you to visit?"* [Set a convenient day and time for you the visit.]
>
> *"Great, I look forward to showing you our homes and community. Would you like for me to call or email you a reminder?"* [Wait for response.]

Yes — *"Fine. I'll send you a note on <mention the specific day> to remind you of our appointment on <mention the day and time>. Which email address should I use?"* [Confirm the address or write it down as you obtain it.]

"See you then. Goodbye."

No — *"Fine. I'll plan on seeing you then <day and time>. Goodbye."*

Does not want to visit — *"That's fine. If you do meet anyone that you think should know about our community (homes), you can either stop by with them or call for an appointment. Either way, I'll be happy to work with you."*

"I'll call you in a few weeks just to let you know how things are progressing at <name of your community or company> and to see how you're doing."

"I really appreciate your help."

"Great seeing you again. Goodbye."

Visit With Your Regular Delivery People

Use this scenario to talk with delivery people that you know because you are their customer or on their route — UPS, FedEx, USPS, office supply, bottled water, coffee service, or other messenger, freight, or parcel delivery service that visit your office on a regular basis — to ask for their help. You may not be able to accomplish that much due to their delivery schedules that they have to keep, so an ensuing phone call or email — or waiting until the next visit — might be required.

———

"Hi, <first name of delivery person that you see on a regular basis>."

[You may not have much time for small talk due to their schedules. If you do fine, but be prepared to get right to your message.]

"I'd like your help on (with) something."

"As you may know (probably know), we're offering here <a basic description of number and style of homes> from <price range>."

"We have some homes ready now for immediate occupancy (will have some ready <date>)."

"Would you like (Do you have time) to take a look at our model while you're here to get a better idea of what we're offering so you can tell others about us?"

Yes — *"Great."* [Determine if they'd like to go by themselves or if they'll allow you to show them around.]

[Since there is not a true interest being conveyed by them and it's you asking for their help, it's OK for them to look on their own. They may feel more in control of their time that way since they still have other stops to make.]

No — *"That's quite all right."* [Regardless of their response and whether or not they go through the model, resume your conversation.]

"I wondered who you might know or might have heard of in your travels who is in the market for a different home that should take a look at what we have to offer." [Wait for response.]

[They may need to let you know later or require some time to think about it, but if he or she readily volunteers a name or two now, write it down and ask for a way to contact them. Be sure to note the correct spelling and pronunciation. Get first names so you don't sound like a telemarketer or solicitor, and get permission to use the person's name that is giving you the referrals when you contact the other people.]

They Have Names to Give You — *"That's great. I will call them and invite them to take a look at what we offer here at <name of your community or company>."*

"The next time you drop by I'll let you know what happened."

"Can you think of anyone else?" [Wait for response.]

"Thanks. I appreciate your help."

"See you next time. Have a great day."

"By the way, if you don't mind, let me give you some of my business cards so you'll have them available if you're talking to anyone that you think should see what we're building. If you can, let me who you give them to."

"Thanks again. Goodbye."

No Names to Give You at This Time — *"That's quite all right. Thanks for trying. Maybe next time."*

"If anyone comes to mind that you think should know about our community (homes), you can tell them about what we're doing, or you can let me know who they are whenever you come in and I'll invite them to come and take a look."

"In fact, if you don't mind, let me give you some of my business cards so you'll have them available if you're talking to anyone that you think should see what we're building. If you can, let me who you give them to."

"I really appreciate your help. See you again next time. Have a good one. Goodbye.

Visit With Your Regular
Service & Repair People

Use this scenario to talk with people you know who visit your office on a regular basis to ask for their help during one of their visits to your office. This would include your computer technician, copier repair technician, regular phone technician or electrician, the people who take care of your indoor plants, the outside landscapers and yard service, the cleaning crew, and other service or technical people that work with you and your company on a regular basis You may not be able to accomplish much during a single conversation due to their schedules, so a subsequent phone call or email — or waiting until their next visit — might be required.

———

"Hi, <first name of service or repair person that you see on a regular basis>."

"I'd like your help on (with) something."

"As you may (probably) know, we're offering here <a basic description of number and style of homes> from <price range>, and we have some homes ready now for immediate occupancy (will have some ready <date>)."

"Would you like (Do you have time) to take a look at our model while you're here to get a better idea of what we're offering so you can tell others about us?"

Yes — *"Great."* [Determine if they'd like to go by themselves or if they'll allow you to show them around.]

[Since there is not a true interest being conveyed by them and it's you asking for their help, it's OK for them to look on their own. They may feel more in control of their time that way since they still have other stops to make.]

No — *"That's quite all right."*

[Regardless of their response and whether or not they go through the model, resume your conversation.]

"I wondered who you might know or might have heard of in your travels who is in the market for a different home that should take a look at what we have to offer." [Wait for a response.]

[They may need to let you know later or require some time to think about it, but if he or she readily volunteers a name or two now, write it down and ask for a way to contact them. Be sure to note the correct spelling and pronunciation. Get first names so you don't sound like a telemarketer or solicitor, and get permission to use the person's name that is giving you the referrals, when you contact the other people.]

They Have Names to Give You — *"That's great. I will call them and invite them to take a look at what we* *offer here at <name of your community or company>. The next time you drop by I'll let you know what happened."*

"Can you think of anyone else?" [Wait for response.]

"Thanks. I appreciate your help. See you next time."

"Have a great day."

"By the way, if you don't mind, let me give you some of my business cards so you'll have them available if you're talking to anyone that you think should see what we're building. If you can, let me who you give them to."

"Thanks again. Goodbye."

No Names to Give You at This Time — *"That's quite all right. Thanks for trying. Maybe another time."*

"If anyone comes to mind that you think should know about our community (homes), you can tell them about what we're doing, or you can let me know who they are whenever you come in and I'll invite them to come and take a look."

"In fact, if you don't mind, let me give you some of my business cards so you'll have them available if you're talking to anyone that you think should see what we're

offering here. If you can, let me know who you give them to."

"I really appreciate your help. See you again next time."

"Have a good one. Goodbye."

Conversation With Your Building Tradespeople

Use this scenario to talk with someone that you have met and already know who has been working on the actual construction of your model or new homes to ask for their help. This could include any of the trades, craftsmen, or installers — from cement masons and finishers to roofing, siding, interior framing and trim, plumbing, electrical, cabinets, flooring, painting, and anything else that goes into the construction and completion of your homes. You may not be able to accomplish much while they're on the job. A subsequent phone call or email — or waiting until their shift is completed — might be required. You might need to set a time to talk with them on their next shift.

———

"Hi, <first name of the craftsman, carpenter, painter, plumber, roofer, electrician, flooring installer, drywall installer, landscaper, that is working on your model and/or new homes>."

"I'd like your help on something."

"As you probably know, we're offering <basic description of number and style of homes> from <price range>."

"Thanks to your efforts and the other members of our team, we have some homes ready now (will have some ready for occupancy in <month>). Your contribution is greatly appreciated. You (you guys) do a great (fantastic) job."

"What I was wondering is who you might know or might have heard of who is in the market for a different home that should take a look at what you're helping to create here. Maybe a friend, or neighbor, or someone else in your company?" [Wait for the response.]

[If he or she readily volunteers a name or two, write it down and ask for a way to contact that person or persons. Be sure to note the correct spelling and pronunciation. Get first names so you don't sound like a telemarketer or solicitor, and get permission to use the person's name that is giving you the referrals when you contact the other people.]

They Have Names to Give You — *"That's great. I will call them and invite them to take a look at what we offer here at <name of your community or company>.*

"I'll let you know what happened when I see you again."

"Can you think of anyone else?" [Wait for response.]

"Thanks for your help. I really appreciate it."

"Have a great day. Goodbye."

No Names to Give You at This Time — *"That's quite all right. Thanks for trying. Maybe another time."*

"By the way, if anyone comes to mind that you think should know about our homes, you can tell them about what we're doing, or you can let me know who they are and I'll invite them to come and take a look."

"Thanks for your time. Keep up the good work. I really appreciate your help and your contribution to our success. I know our customers will, too."

"Have a good day. Goodbye."

Conversation With Your Building Professionals

Use this scenario to talk with someone that you know who has been involved in working on the actual design, construction, and completion of your model or new homes — to ask for their help. This could include your architects, interior designers, decorators, stagers, surveyors, inspectors, engineers, consultants, landscape architects, attorneys, title companies, appraisers, lenders, or anyone else that you know who worked with you and your company. You may not be able to accomplish that much while they're there on business so an ensuing phone call or email might be required — or waiting until the next time they visit.

"Hi, <first name of architect, engineer, landscape architect, interior decorator, designer, consultant, lender, appraiser, attorney, or others that are working on your model or new homes>."

"I'd like your help on something."

"Thanks to your efforts and the others on our team, we are offering some really great homes. What I was wondering is who you might know or might have heard of who is in the market for a different home that should take a look at what you're helping to create here." [Wait for the response.]

[If he or she readily volunteers a name or two, write it down and ask for a way to contact that person or persons. Be sure to note the correct spelling and pronunciation. Get first names so you don't sound like a telemarketer or solicitor, and get permission to use the person's name that is giving you the referrals when you contact the other people.]

They Have Names to Give You — *"That's great."*

"I will call them and invite them to take a look at what we offer here at <name of your community or company>. The next time I see you I'll let you know what happened."

"Can you think of anyone else?" [Wait for response.]

"Thanks for your help. I really appreciate it."

"In fact, if you don't mind, let me give you some of my business cards so you'll have them available if you're talking to anyone that you think should see what we're building. If you can, let me who you give them to."

"Have a great day. Goodbye."

No Names to Give You at This Time — *"That's quite all right. Thanks for trying. Maybe another time."*

"By the way, if anyone comes to mind that you think should know about our homes, you can tell them about what we're doing, or you can let me know who they are and I'll invite them to come and take a look."

"In fact, if you don't mind, let me give you some of my business cards so you'll have them available if you're talking to anyone that you think should see what we're building. If you can, let me who you give them to."

"Thanks for your time. Keep up the good work. Nice talking with you today."

"I really appreciate your help and your contribution to our success. I know our customers will, too."

"Have a good day. Goodbye."

Conversation With People At A Special Event Or Trade Show

Use this scenario to talk with someone you have talked with and already gotten to know briefly who has just finished looking at your homes or display during a special event like the Parade of Homes, a grand opening, an off-site display like a kiosk, or a trade show or home expo. Whether they seem to have a specific interest in your homes or not, ask for their help to determine if there are others that they can lead you to who should look at or know about your homes.

———

[After discussing your homes, answering their questions, conducting your discovery, and engaging in small talk, turn the conversation to this — whether any additional contact has been set with them.]

"Many people, after they see (hear about) what we have to offer, say, 'Gee, I wish so-and-so could see this. This would be perfect for them (for what they are looking for),' or 'I wish Fred and Linda had been here to see this. This is exactly the type of home they're looking for (interested in).'"

[Look to see if they nod agreement or indicate that they have been feeling this sentiment.]

"Who comes to mind that you've been thinking this about as I have been talking with you about our homes?" [Wait for a response.]

[If they volunteer a name or two, write it down and ask for a way to contact that person or persons. Be sure to note the correct spelling and pronunciation. Get first names so you don't sound like a telemarketer or solicitor, and get permission to use the person's name that is giving you the referrals when you contact the other people. If your company offers an incentive for referrals, discuss this inducement for providing names.]

They Have Names to Give You — *"That's great. I will call them and invite them to take a look at what we offer here at <name of your community or company>."*

"Can you think of anyone else?" [Wait for response.]

"Thanks for your help. I really appreciate it."

"In fact, if you don't mind, let me give you some of my business cards so you'll have them available if you're talking to anyone that you think should see what we're building. Just have them mention your name when they contact me or let me know who they are. If you like, you can call (email) me to tell me who to watch for."

[Continue with your presentation, including setting and agreeing on the next contact.]

No Names to Give You at This Time — *"That's quite all right. Thanks for trying."*

"By the way, if anyone comes to mind that you think should know about our homes, you can tell me the next time we talk and I'll invite them to take a look."

"In fact, if you don't mind, let me give you some of my business cards so you'll have them available if you're talking to anyone that you think should see what we're building. Just have them mention your name when they contact me or let me know who they are. If you like, you can call (email) me to tell me who to watch for."

[Continue with your presentation, including setting and agreeing on the next contact.]

Conversation With Interested People After An On-Site Presentation

Use this scenario to talk with someone who has just finished looking at your homes with you and seems to like what they have seen — to ask for their help while they're still onsite with you. You want to determine if there are other people that they can lead you to who should look at your homes.

———

[After showing the model or available homesites and conducting the bulk of your presentation, turn your conversation toward asking for referrals.]

"Many people, after they see what we have to offer, say, 'Gee, I wish so-and-so could see this. This would be perfect for them (for what they are looking for)' or 'I wish Fred and Linda had been here with us to see this. This is exactly the type of home they're looking for (interested in).'" [Look to see if they nod agreement.]

"Who have you been saying this about as I have been showing you our homes?" [Wait for a response.]

[If they volunteer a name or two, write it down and ask for a way to contact that person or persons. Be sure to note the correct spelling and pronunciation. Get first names so you don't sound like a telemarketer or solicitor, and get permission to use the person's name that is giving you the referrals when you contact the other people. If your company offers an incentive for referrals, discuss this inducement for providing names.]

They Have Names to Give You — *"That's great. I will call them and invite them to take a look at what we offer here at <name of your community or company>."*

"The next time we talk, I'll let you know what they had to say and if they seemed to like what we are offering as much as you think they will."

"Can you think of anyone else?" [Wait for response.]

"Thanks for your help. I really appreciate it. "

[Continue with your presentation, including setting and agreeing on the next contact.]

"In fact, if you don't mind, let me give you some of my business cards so you'll have them available if you're talking to anyone that you think should see what we're building. Just have them mention your name when they contact me or let me know who they are. If you like, you can call (email) me to tell me who to watch for."

"Goodbye. " [Remind them of your next contact.]

No Names to Give You at This Time — *"That's quite all right. Thanks for trying. Maybe the next time we talk. "*

"By the way, if anyone comes to mind that you think should know about our homes, you can tell me the next time we talk and I'll invite them to come and take a look."

[Continue with your presentation, including setting and agreeing on the next contact.]

"In fact, if you don't mind, let me give you some of my business cards so you'll have them if you're talking to anyone that you think should see what we're building. "

"Just have them mention your name when they contact me or let me know who they are. If you like, you can call (email) me to tell me who to watch for."

"Goodbye." [Remind them of your next contact.]

Conversation With Uninterested People After An On-Site Presentation

Use this scenario to talk with someone who has just finished looking at your homes with you that does not like or can't use what you offer — you can still ask for their help because they can lead you to others.

———

[After conducting your sales presentation, but prior to saying goodbye to them, turn your conversation toward asking for referrals.]

"I really have enjoyed our time together today, and I'm sorry that you don't think we can meet your needs here at <name of your community or company>, but let me ask you this."

"Obviously, different people have different needs, so there's probably at least one person or couple that you can think of right now — or that came to mind as we were looking at our homes — who might like to hear about what we have to offer or really should take a look at what you just saw? [Wait for response.]

"Who have you thought of that you think would enjoy learning about what we offer here at <name of your community or company>?" [Wait for a response.]

[If they volunteer a name or two, write it down and then ask for a way to contact that person or persons. Be sure to note the correct spelling and pronunciation of each name, and get their first names so you don't sound like a telemarketer or solicitor, and get permission to use the person's name that is giving you the referrals when you contact the other people. If your company offers an incentive for referrals, discuss this inducement for providing names.]

They Have Names to Give You — *"That's great. I will call them and invite them to take a look at what we offer here at <your community or company>."*

"Can you think of anyone else?" [Wait for response.]

"Thanks for your help. I really appreciate it."

"In fact, if you don't mind, let me give you some of my business cards so you'll have them available if you're talking to anyone that you think should see what we're building."

"Just have them mention your name when they contact me or let me know who they are. If you like, you can call (email) me to tell me who to watch for."

"Goodbye, and thanks for visiting."

No Names to Give You at This Time — *"That's quite all right. Thanks for trying."*

"By the way, if anyone comes to mind that you think should know about our homes, please let me know."

"In fact, if you don't mind, let me give you some of my business cards so you'll have them available if you're talking to anyone that you think should see what we're building. Just have them mention your name when they contact me or let me know who they are."

"Goodbye, and thanks for visiting."

Conversation With A New Purchaser

Use this scenario to talk with someone who has purchased a new home from you. This can be used at the time of the purchase agreement, while doing selections, at the closing table, or any other time prior to move-in. You are looking for people that they know that they haven't already told about that you can talk to about your new homes.

———

[After discussing the other issues that you needed to address, turn your conversation toward asking for referrals.]

"Now that you have decided that <name of your community or company> is the place for you to live, I am sure that you can think of several of your friends or associates that you would like to have at least look at our homes and perhaps some of them would want to live here with you as well." [Watch for a nod or agreement.]

"Who are the first two or three people who come to mind that you think really ought to look at what we have to offer?" [Wait for a response.]

[Be prepared to write down any names they give you (or give them a card that they can use for this purpose) and ask for a way to contact those people they tell you about that they think might interested in looking at your homes. Be sure to note the correct spelling and pronunciation. Get first names so you don't sound like a telemarketer or solicitor. Get permission to use your purchaser's name(s) when you contact the other people.]

[If your company offers an incentive for referrals — especially from new purchasers, discuss this inducement for providing names.]

They Have Names to Give You — *"That's great."*

"I'll invite them to look at what we have to offer, and I'll let you know what happened."

"Can you think of anyone else?" [Wait for response.]

"Thanks for your help. I really appreciate it." [Continue with your conversation.]

"By the way, let me give you some of my business cards so you'll have them available if you're talking to anyone that you think should see what we're building. Just have them mention your name when they contact me or let me know who they are so I can look out for them. If you like, you can call (email) me to tell me who to watch for, or you can even bring them by."

"Goodbye."

No Names to Give You at This Time — *"That's quite all right.*

"You'll probably think of some later on, and you can tell me about them the next time we talk or even email them to me. Then I'll invite them to visit us and take a look at our homes."

"By the way, let me give you some of my business cards so you'll have them available if you're talking to anyone that you think should see what we're building. Just have them mention your name when they contact me or let me know who they are so I can look out for them. If you like, you can call (email) me to tell me who to watch for, or you can even bring them by."

[Continue with your conversation.] *"Goodbye."*

Alternate Conversation
With A New Purchaser

Use this scenario as another way of talking with someone in-person who is buying a new home from you — as they go through the purchasing process with you but before they actually take possession and move into it. You are looking for referrals.

———

[After discussing the other issues that you need to address, turn your conversation toward asking for referrals.]

"Since you have selected a home in an area of <name of your community or neighborhood> that still has several available homesites, you might like to help choose some of your new neighbors (help us select some of your new neighbors)."

"Who are the first three or four names (people, friends) who come to mind that you think you'd like to have living near you or alongside you in your new neighborhood?" [Wait for a response.]

[Be prepared to write down any names they give you and ask for a way to contact those people. Be sure to note the correct spelling and pronunciation. Get first names so you don't sound like a telemarketer or solicitor. Get permission to use your purchaser's name(s) when you contact the other people. If your company offers an incentive to customers for referrals, discuss this inducement.]

They Have Names to Give You — *"That's great. I'll invite them to look at what we have to offer, and the next time we talk I'll let you know what happened."*

"Can you think of anyone else?" [Wait for response.]

"Thanks for your help. I really appreciate it, and I think they will, too."

"By the way, let me give you some of my business cards so you'll have them available if you're talking to anyone that you think should see what we're building or you want to arrange to show them your new home. Just have them mention your name when they contact me or let me know who they are so I'll be sure to look out for them. If you like, you can call (email) me to tell me who to watch for, or you can even bring them by."

[Continue with your conversation.] *"Goodbye."*

No Names to Give You at This Time — *"That's quite all right."*

"You'll probably think of some later on, and you can tell me about them the next time we talk or you can email them to me."

"Then I'll invite them to visit us and take a look at our homes."

"By the way, let me give you some of my business cards so you'll have them available if you're talking to anyone that you think should see what we're building or you want to arrange to show them your new home. Just have them mention your name when they contact me or let me know who they are so I'll be sure to look out for them. If you like, you can call (email) me to tell me who to watch for, or you can even bring them by."

[Continue with your conversation.] *"Goodbye."*

Conversation With A New Resident

Use this scenario to approach and talk with someone that has recently moved into a new home you sold them. There's no certain time to wait, but this should be after your initial move-in day visit. You might see them outside washing the car, gardening, walking the dog, getting the mail, watching the kids, playing catch, sitting on their porch, or cutting the grass — or you might make a special visit to their new home. You are interested in their adjustment into their new home and in referring their friends to you since they should like the location and you.

———

[Greet them and exchange small talk. Compliment them

on their landscaping or something else that catches your eye.] *"I hope that things are going well for you in your new home and that you're getting settled."*

[If there are any issues, deal with them as you can. You want them to be happy because this will help with your referrals, but you are not there for warranty issues. Keep the conversation away from that if possible.]

"As you're getting acquainted with the joys of living here at <name of your community or company or neighborhood>, I'm sure that you have had a chance to think of several people that really ought to know about what we offer — even if they don't actually decide to live here."

"Who are the first three or four names (friends, people) that you've been thinking about as people (ones) who ought to know what we have to offer?"

"I would be happy to call them for you and let them know that I'm available at their convenience to show them what we have and see what they might think." [Wait for a response.]

[If they volunteer a name or two, write it down and ask for a way to contact that person or persons. Be sure to note the correct spelling and pronunciation. Get first names so you don't sound like a telemarketer or solicitor, and get permission to use your new resident's name when you contact the other people. If your company offers an incentive to customers for referring others, mention this as an inducement for providing names.]

They Have Names to Give You — *"That's great. The next time we talk I'll let you know what happened."*

"Can you think of anyone else?" [Wait for response.]

"Thanks for your help. I really appreciate it."

"By the way, let me give you some of my business cards so you'll have them available if you're talking to anyone that you think should see what we're building here. Just have them mention your name when they contact me or let me know who they are so I'll be sure to look out for them. If you like, you can call (email, stop by) to tell me who to watch for, or you can even bring them by."

[Continue with your conversation.] *"Good luck with your new home, and let me know if I can help out in anyway. Goodbye."*

No Names to Give You at This Time — *"That's quite all right. Thanks for trying."*

"I'm sure you'll probably think of some people later on, and you can tell me who they are the next time we talk — or you can drop by the office or email the names to me. Then I'll contact them and invite them to visit us."

"By the way, let me give you some of my business cards so you'll have them available if you're talking to anyone that you think should see what we're building. Just have them mention your name when they contact me or let me know who they are so I'll be sure to look out for them. If you like, you can call (email, stop by) to tell me who to watch for, or you can even bring them by."

[Continue with your conversation.] *"Good luck with your new home, and let me know if I can help out in anyway. Goodbye."*

Alternate Conversation With A New Resident

Use this scenario as another way of talking with someone who recently moved into a new home you sold them and for asking for their help in identifying people you should talk with about your new homes.

———

[Greet them and exchange small talk. Compliment them on an aspect of their home such as their landscaping.]

"Since you have selected a home on a street that still has several available homesites, you might like to help choose some of your new neighbors (help us select some of your new neighbors)."

"Who are the first three or four names (people, friends)

who come to mind that you'd like to have (you think would like to have) live on your new street along with you?" [Wait for a response.]

[Be prepared to write down any names they give you and ask for a way to contact those people. Be sure to note the correct spelling and pronunciation. Get first names so you don't sound like a telemarketer or solicitor. Get permission to use your purchaser's name(s) when you contact the other people. If your company offers an incentive to customers for referrals, discuss this inducement for providing names.]

They Have Names to Give You — *"That's great. I'll invite them to look at what we have to offer, and the next time we talk I'll let you know what happened."*

"Can you think of anyone else?" [Wait for response.]

"Thanks for your help. I really appreciate it."

"By the way, let me give you some of my business cards so you'll have them available if you're talking to anyone that you think should see what we're building here. Just have them mention your name when they contact me or let me know who they are so I'll be sure to look out for them. If you like, you can call (email, stop by) to tell me who to watch for, or you can even bring them by."

[Continue with your conversation.] *"Good luck with your new home."*

"Please let me know if I can help out in anyway. Goodbye."

No Names to Give You at This Time — *"That's quite all right. Thanks for trying."*

"I'm sure you'll think of some people later on, and you can tell me who they are the next time we talk — or you can email them to me or drop by the office. Then I'll contact them and invite them to take a look at what we have."

"By the way, let me give you some of my business cards so you'll have them available if you're talking to anyone that you think should see what we're building here. Just have them mention your name when they contact me or let me know who they are so I'll be sure to look out for them. If you like, you can call (email, stop by) to tell me who to watch for, or you can even bring them by."

[Continue with your conversation.] *"Good luck with your new home. Please let me know if I can help you in anyway. Goodbye."*

Conversation With An Established Resident

Use this scenario to talk with someone that has been a resident of your community for several months that you have already met. You might see them outside washing the car, gardening, trimming the bushes, walking the dog, getting the mail, watching the kids, playing catch, sitting on their porch, doing some exterior maintenance, painting, or cutting the grass — or you might make a special visit to their new home to talk about how you can use their help.

———

[Greet them and exchange small talk. Pick out something specific to highlight or compliment them on.]

"I really appreciate the confidence you have shown in us by owning one of our homes. It means a lot to me, and I really could use your help."

"As you probably know from driving around the community, we have several great homesites available, and I'd love for you to have some of your friends join you in living here and enjoying all that we have to offer."

"Who are the first two or three names that come to mind that you think would like to live here in <name of your community> along with you?" [Wait for a response.]

[Be prepared to write down any names they give you and ask for a way to contact those people. Be sure to note the correct spelling and pronunciation. Get first names so you don't sound like a telemarketer or solicitor. Get permission to use your resident's name(s) when you contact the other people. If your company offers an incentive to residents for referrals, discuss this inducement for providing names.]

They Have Names to Give You — *"That's great. I'll invite them to look at what we have to offer, and the next time we talk I'll let you know what happened."*

"Can you think of anyone else?" [Wait for response.]

"Thanks for your help. I really appreciate it."

"By the way, let me give you some of my business cards so you'll have them available if you're talking to anyone that you think should see what we offer. Just have them mention your name when they contact me or let me know who they are so I'll be sure to look out for them. If you like, you can call (email, stop by) to tell me who to watch for, or you can even bring them by."

[Continue with your conversation.] *"Goodbye. Have a great day."*

No Names to Give You at This Time — *"That's quite all right. Thanks for trying. Maybe another time."*

"I'm sure you'll think of some people later on, and you can tell me who they are the next time we talk or you can drop by the office or email me. Then I'll contact them and invite them to take a look at what we have so they can experience what you already know."

"By the way, let me give you some of my business cards so you'll have them available if you're talking to anyone that you think should see what we offer. Just have them mention your name when they contact me or let me know who they are so I'll be sure to look out for them. If you like, you can call (email, stop by) to tell me who to watch for, or you can even bring them by."

[Continue with your conversation.] *"Goodbye and have a great day."*

Alternate Conversation With An Established Resident

Use this scenario as another way of talking with someone who has been a resident of your community for several months that you have already met — to ask for their help in identifying people you should talk with about your new homes.

[Greet them and exchange small talk. Pick out something specific to compliment them on or highlight.]

"I really appreciate the confidence you have shown in us by owning one of our homes. It means a lot to me, and I really could use your help."

"As you probably know from driving around the community, we are nearly finished building new homes in here. In fact

the homesite next to you (across the street, just down the block from you) is one of the few homesites (the only one) remaining. I'd love for you to have one of your friends join you in living here and enjoying all that we have to offer."

"Who comes to mind that you think would like to live here in <name of your community> along with you?" [Wait for a response.]

[Be prepared to write down any names they give you and ask for a way to contact those people. Be sure to note the correct spelling and pronunciation. Get first names so you don't sound like a telemarketer or solicitor. Get permission to use your resident's name(s) when you contact the other people. If your company offers an incentive to residents for referrals, discuss this inducement for providing names.]

They Have Names to Give You — "That's great. I'll invite them to look at what we have to offer, and I'll bring them by to see you when they're here."

"Thanks for your help. I really appreciate it."

"By the way, let me give you a few of my business cards so you'll have them available if you're talking to anyone that you think should see what we offer. Just have them mention your name when they contact me or let me know who they are so I'll be sure to look out for them. If you like, you can call (email, stop by) to tell me who

to watch for, or you can even bring them by. Just keep
in mind that we just have the few (one) remaining."

[Continue with your conversation.] "Goodbye. Have a
great day."

No Names to Give You at This Time — "That's quite all
right. Thanks for trying."

"If you think of anyone later on, be sure to let me know
who it is so I can contact them and invite them to take a
look at what we offer so they can experience what you
already know."

"By the way, let me give you a few of my business cards
so you'll have them available if you're talking to anyone
that you think should see what we offer. Just have them
mention your name when they contact me or let me
know who they are so I'll be sure to look out for them.
If you like, you can call (email, stop by) to tell me who
to watch for, or you can even bring them by. Just keep
in mind that we just have the few (one) remaining."

[Continue with your conversation.] "Goodbye and have a
great day."

Conversation With A Referring Resident

Use this scenario to talk with someone that has been a
resident of your community for a number of months that

you already have met — to thank them for furnishing you with leads in the past and to request their help again.

––––––

[Greet them and exchange small talk. Pick out something specific to compliment them on or highlight.]

"I really value your trust and confidence that you have shown in us by owning one of our homes. It means a lot to me."

"You've already given me the names of several (many, one, two, a couple) of your friends (former neighbors, relatives, co-workers, associates) and have allowed me to contact them to let them know about the opportunities available here at <your community or your company>."

"I really appreciate your help, but I still can use your assistance."

"We all meet new people all the time — or think of ones that we hadn't thought of before — so in addition to your friends (former neighbors, relatives, co-workers, associates, colleagues, clients) that you've already told me about, I thought I'd check with you to see which two or three people you might have met recently or that you hadn't thought about before that you think should know about what we offer here at <name of your community or your company>." [Wait for response.]

[Be prepared to write down any names they give you and ask for a way to contact those people. Be sure to note the correct spelling and pronunciation. Get first names so you don't sound like a telemarketer or solicitor. Get permission to use your resident's name(s) when you contact the other people. If your company offers an incentive for referrals, discuss this — especially if it's a new policy.]

They Have Names to Give You — *"That's great. I'll invite them like I did the others you told me about to look at what we have to offer. The next time we talk I'll let you know what happened."*

"Can you think of anyone else?" [Wait for response.]

"Thanks for your help. I really appreciate it."

"By the way, let me give you some of my business cards so you'll have them available if you're talking to anyone that you think should see what we offer. Just let me know who they are so I'll be sure to look out for them. If you like, you can call (email, stop by) to tell me who to watch for, or you can even bring them by."

[Continue with your conversation.] *"Goodbye and have a great day."*

No Names to Give You at This Time — *"That's quite all right. Thanks for trying. Maybe the next time."*

"I'm sure you'll probably think of some more people later on, and you can tell me who they are the next time we talk or you can drop by the office or email me (give me a call)."

"Then I'll contact them like I did before and invite them to take a look at what we have."

"By the way, let me give you some of my business cards so you'll have them available if you're talking to anyone that you think should see what we offer. Just let me know who they are so I'll be sure to look out for them. If you like, you can call (email, stop by) to tell me who to watch for, or you can even bring them by."

[Continue with your conversation.] *"Goodbye and have a great day."*

5

Connecting By Telephone

The Value Of Telephone Contact

Planned, or even impromptu, in-person meetings and conversations are great for interacting and connecting with friends and acquaintances.

Smiles, shrugs, hand gestures, grins, chuckles, laughs, raised eyebrows, a touch, rolling of the eyes, surprised or shocked looks, anger, disgust, frustration, elation, frowns, confusion, empathy, and other expressions of emotion are immediately conveyed during a face-to-face meeting or conversation.

However, that type of contact — as ideal as it is — isn't always necessary, available, or convenient. The person you want to talk with could be hundreds or even thousands of miles away.

Therefore, the next best thing to talking to someone in-person is speaking to them by phone.

The telephone is a powerful way of reaching out and staying connected with your circle of contacts.

While you can't see what each other is saying and how you are communicating your message (unless you're using something like Skype, FaceTime, or webcams), you still get to hear each other and often can sense how the other is speaking — particularly if you know them fairly well.

Your "Circle Of Contacts"

All of us know people from a variety of sources — family, school, former employers and employees, colleagues, customers, current and former neighborhoods, church, clubs, organizations, community and civic groups, recreational activities, charities, local businesses and professionals, and friends of our kids and spouse.

Many people refer to this network of friends, family, and associates that we have as our "sphere of influence," but I don't think this is a great term to use.

Rather, I use a more inclusive term that applies to all the people we know — regardless of how we met them, how well we might know them, how long we have known them, and when we last spoke to them. I simply call it our "circle of contacts."

Undoubtedly, you have a database of your contacts stored as a stack of business cards in your rolodex or in a drawer, a more formal arrangement of them in your computer in a CRM (contact relational manager, such as ACT! or Outlook), in your PDA, on your smartphone, or on more than one of these.

Anytime you want, you can pick up the telephone and reach out to any of your contacts. You probably even have the numbers of the people you call the most memorized, on speed dial, or in your list of favorites.

The nice thing about using the phone to contact people is that you don't have to get in your car or leave your home or office. No special preparation is required other than what you want to say and who you want to call.

You Know Many People

In addition to your family, neighbors, close friends, colleagues, associates, and others you see or socialize with on a regular basis, there are many other business contacts that you can rely upon to help you generate leads and build your business.

These include other salespeople in your market that you have a good relationship with and that you're not in direct competition with, brokers that you know — even if they haven't visited your community, professional contacts such as attorneys and physicians that you know in your market area, and lenders and mortgage brokers that you have worked with.

You also have names and phone numbers for appraisers, home inspectors, interior decorators, home stagers, suppliers, tradespeople, businesses that you patronize, entertainment and recreational facilities you use, governmental offices where you know people, and restaurants in your area that you patronize.

Add to that the customers you've sold homes to and the ones you're still working with to help them find their perfect home.

Your data bank is full of names and phone numbers.

Getting Started

All you need to do is begin tapping into this major resource as you reach out and connect with people you already know and ask for their help.

You need referrals, and they can help you. They want to help you. You just need to ask and make them aware of what you need.

We already addressed calling on people in-person or seeing them in public. This chapter focuses specifically on using the telephone to connect with people that you already know in some way.

I'm talking specifically about connecting by phone with people that you already know and that you know well enough — even if you haven't seen or spoken with them in a while — to be able to pick up the phone, call them, and have them take your call and speak with you.

There's nothing to be apprehensive about.

You're calling your friends, people who know you, or those who recognize your name well enough to take your call and speak with you.

Not everyone may agree to help or feel that they are capable of helping you, but your request is legitimate and is not based on testing or taking advantage of your friendship.

Tapping Into A Willingness

In this chapter, I give you some suggested language to use for your telephone conversations as you reach out to people that can help you. Use it as is or as a guide.

Just remember that the people you are calling are not strangers. Some you will know better than others, and some longer than others. However, there is no reason not to call them and ask for their help.

People like to help you if they know what you need and feel that it's something they can do.

It's human nature to want to help someone if we feel that we can and that we won't be too inconvenienced by doing so.

You just need to ask the people you're calling for their help and make them aware of what you need. Then reassure them that they have the ability to help you.

Call After A Brief Introduction

Use this scenario for your telephone call the day after or soon after meeting someone initially and talking briefly with them at a business or social function or in public. Primarily you want to talk with them some more or set up a meeting with them to determine if they have an interest in what you offer and who they might know that has an interest in buying a new home.

———

"Hello <use their first name>?"

"This is <your name> from <name of your community or company — or both (whichever the person you're calling will recognize)>."

"I met you <last night, Tuesday, yesterday, the other day, last week, or recently> at the <mention the specific event or place where you met, such as Chamber of Commerce breakfast, church, Little League game, the mall, a specific store or restaurant, the Rotary Club,

etc.> and we met just long enough to exchange business cards and that was about it."

"Do you have a quick minute?" [Wait for response.]

NOW IS NOT A GOOD TIME — [You actually speak to your new friend or acquaintance, but they are unable to devote any additional time to you now.] *"No problem. Let me call back when you have a minute."*

"I just wanted to call to say hello again and to set a convenient (good) time when I could stop by to meet with you for a few minutes." [Set up a convenient time to talk again, but do not set the appointment to meet at this time unless they insist and will talk long enough to set the future appointment but no more.] *"Goodbye."*

HAS JUST A QUICK MINUTE NOW — [You actually get to speak to the person you are calling, but they don't have much time to talk — just set an appointment for the next contact.] *"Great. I'll make this quick."*

"I just wanted to call to say hello again and to set a convenient (good) time when I could stop by for a couple of minutes to learn a little bit more about your business (what you do) and let you know who we are."

"Maybe you'd let me buy you a cup of coffee. Which one is better for you <meeting at their office or a coffee shop>?" [Wait for response.]

"Fine." [Agree on the place, date, and time].

"Thanks. I look forward to seeing you again on <date of the appointment> at <agreed time> at <agreed location>."

"Would you like for me to email you a reminder?" [Wait for response.]

> **Yes** — *"Fine. I'll send you a note on <specific day> to remind you of our appointment on <day, time, and location>. Which email address should I use?"* [Confirm the address or write it down as you obtain it.]
>
> *"I look forward to seeing (meeting) you then. Goodbye."*
>
> **No** — *"Fine. I'll plan on seeing you then on <mention the day and time> at <place>. Goodbye."*

Call To A Social Networking Contact

Use this scenario to call any person that you know through social networking sites because you have commented on their site or connected with them online sufficiently that they know who you are. You mainly want to talk with them — rather than set a meeting — to determine who they know who has an interest in buying a new home and who they can refer to you. Call them on their cell phone to avoid office voice mail and "screeners." They may be miles away from your area.

"Hello <use their first name>? This is <your name>."

"I know you from <name of networking site where you both are a member>. [The person you are calling should immediately recognize your name.]

NOW IS NOT A GOOD TIME — *"No problem. I know you weren't expecting my call right now. Let me call back when you have a minute."* [Set up a convenient time to talk again.]

"I'll give you a call again on <date agreed, and possibly set a specific time as well>. Goodbye."

IS AVAILABLE NOW — *"Great. I'll make this fairly quick."*

"As you may (probably) know, I sell new homes in <name of your area or town>. I thought maybe you could help me identify people who might be interested in looking for a new home in my area — now or in the near future.

[Listen for their general willingness to help you. If he or she mentions that they would like to help, set up another call at a mutually convenient time. If they volunteer a name or two, write it down and ask for a way to contact that person or persons. Be sure to note the correct spelling and pronunciation. Get first names so you don't sound like a telemarketer or solicitor when you call them, and get permission to use their name when you contact the other people. If there seems to be no interest in helping you or in establishing a professional relationship, conclude the call.]

"Thanks for taking my call. Goodbye. See you online."

Call To A Friend Or Acquaintance

Use this scenario to call and talk with someone you know very well or well enough to speak to each other and have a conversation when you meet. You want to make sure they know what your current role is and that you want to enlist their help in identifying people that they know that might be interested in looking at or purchasing a new home such as you offer.

———

"Hi, <first name or nickname of your friend>. This is <your name — possibly just your first name>."

"I wasn't sure if you were aware that I am (began) working with <name of your company or community — or both> and we're located at <a general description is probably enough>."

"I'd really like to catch up with you and learn more about your business and what you do and get a chance to tell you about what we are doing. Also, I possibly could use your help."

"Do you have some now or would it be better for me to call back at a better time?" [Wait for response.]

Now Is OK — *"Fine."* [Discuss what your friend is doing. You also can set a time to get together for breakfast or coffee depending on how close your offices are to each other. Then talk about your homes and what you are doing. Listen for an indication of interest.]

"I mentioned that I can use your help. I thought maybe you could help me identify people who might be interested in looking for a new home in my area — now or in the near future. Possibly some people that you know that I don't."

"Who are the first couple of names that come to mind right now that you think would take my call to let them know about our homes?" [Wait for response.]

[If they volunteer a name or two, write it down and ask for a way to contact that person or persons. Be sure to note the correct spelling and pronunciation. Get first names so you don't sound like a telemarketer or solicitor when you call them, and get permission to use their name when you contact the other people. If your company offers an incentive for referrals, discuss this inducement for providing names.]

"I'd like to send you our newsletter on a periodic basis just so you will be aware of what we're offering. Is email OK?" [Wait for the response. Confirm their email address or determine which one to use. You can also send them your contact information or vCard and send them a link

to your website and blog, if you have one. Then, discuss your next contact and agree on when and where that is to be and if it's by email, phone, or in-person.]

"I'll talk to (see) you again then. Really great talking to you. Thanks for your time. Goodbye."

NOW IS NOT A GOOD TIME — *"I knew that you might be busy and that you weren't expecting my call right now, but I thought I'd take a chance."*

"Let me call back when you have a minute." [Set up a convenient time to talk again.]

"Talk to you then. Goodbye."

Call From A Friend Or Acquaintance

Use this scenario to talk with someone you know very well or well enough to speak to each other and have a conversation when you meet — when they call you about maybe even an unrelated issue. They will be calling you on your cell phone since the presumption is that they don't know where you are working. You might recognize their phone number or their voice. You want to make sure they know what your current role is and that you want to enlist their help in identifying people that they know that might be interested in looking at or purchasing a new home such as you offer.

———

[Answer the phone. Hear the other person identify themself.] *"Hi, <first name or nickname of your friend>."* [Listen to them and discuss what they want to talk about with you. Then at an appropriate moment, change gears and use the conversation to talk about what you want.]

"I recently began working with <name of your company or community — or both> and we're located at <a general description is probably enough>." [Talk briefly about your homes and what you offer.]

"You know, I could really use your help. Do you have another minute now or would it be better for me to give you a call later?" [Wait for response.]

Now Is OK — *"Fine. I thought maybe you could help me identify some people who might be interested in looking for a new home in my area — now or in the near future. Possibly some people that you know that I don't."*

"Who are the first couple of names that come to mind right now that you think would take my call to let them know about our homes?" [Wait for response.]

[If they volunteer a name or two, write it down and ask for a way to contact that person or persons. Be sure to note the correct spelling and pronunciation. Get first names so you don't sound like a telemarketer or solicitor when you call them, and get permission to use their name when you contact the other people. If your company offers an incentive for referrals, discuss this inducement for providing names.]

"I'd like to send you our newsletter on a periodic basis just so you will be aware of what we're offering. Is email OK?" [Wait for the response. Confirm their email address or determine which one to use. You can also send them your contact information or vCard and send them a link to your website and blog, if you have one.]

[Discuss your next contact and agree on when and where that is to be and if it's by email, phone, or in-person. You might set a time to get together for breakfast or coffee depending on how close your offices are to each other.]

"I'll talk to (see) you again then. Really great talking to you. Thanks for the call and your help. Goodbye."

LATER WOULD BE BETTER — *"That's fine. It can wait."* [Set up a convenient time to talk again.] *"Talk to you then. Goodbye."*

Call To An Old Contact

Use this scenario to call and talk with someone you know from your past well enough to speak to each other and have a conversation when you meet — but it's been a long time since you saw or spoke to each other. You want to make sure they know what your current role is and that you want to enlist their help in identifying people that they know that might be interested in looking at or purchasing a new home such as you offer.

———

"Hi, <first name or nickname of your friend>, this is <your name>."

"How have you been? It's been a long time." [Wait for response.]

"We haven't talked in a while so I wanted to make sure that you knew that I am (began) working with <name of your company or community — or both> and we're located at <a general description is probably enough>."

"I wanted to say hello since it's been a while since we talked, but the main reason for my call is that I'd like your help. Do you have a moment now or would it be better for me to call back at a better time?" [Wait for response.]

Now Is OK — *"Fine."* [Talk about your homes briefly so that they have a frame of reference. Listen for any interest they show.]

"I thought maybe you could help me identify people who might be interested in looking for a new home in my area — now or in the near future. Possibly some people that you know that I don't."

"Who are the first couple of names that come to mind right now that you think would take my call to let them know about our homes?" [Wait for response.]

[If they volunteer a name or two, write it down and ask for a way to contact that person or persons. Be sure to note the correct spelling and pronunciation. Get first names so you don't sound like a telemarketer or solicitor when you call them, and get permission to use their name when you contact the other people. If your company offers an incentive for referrals, discuss this inducement for providing names.]

"I'd like to send you our newsletter on a periodic basis just so you will be aware of what we're offering. Is email OK?" [Wait for the response. Confirm their email address or determine which one to use. You can also send them your contact information or vCard and send them a link to your website and blog, if you have one.]

[Discuss your next contact and agree on when and where that is to be and if it's by email, phone, or in-person. You can set a time to re-establish your relationship by getting together for coffee depending on how close your offices are to each other.]

"I'll talk to (see) you then. Really great talking to you again. Thanks for your help. Goodbye."

NOW IS NOT A GOOD TIME — *"I knew that you might be busy*

and that you weren't expecting my call right now, but I thought I'd take a chance. Let me call back when you have a minute." [Set up a convenient time to talk again.] *"Talk to you then. Goodbye."*

Call From An Old Contact

Use this scenario when you get an unexpected call from someone you know from your past well enough to speak to each other and have a conversation when you meet — but it's been a long time since you spoke or saw each other. During this call, you want to make sure they know what your current role is and that you want to enlist their help in identifying people that they know that might be interested in looking at or purchasing a new home such as you offer.

———

[Answer the phone. Hear the other person identify themself.] *"Hi, <first name or nickname of your friend>. Boy, it's been a while. Great to hear from you."*

[Listen to them and discuss what they want to talk with you about. Then at an appropriate moment, change gears and use the conversation to talk about what you want.]

"I'm now working with <name of your company or community — or both> and we're located at <a general description is probably enough>." [Talk briefly about your homes and what you offer.]

"You know, I could really use your help. Do you have another minute now or would it be better for me to give you a call later?" [Wait for response.]

Now Is OK — *"Fine. I thought maybe you could help me identify some people who might be interested in looking for a new home in my area — now or in the near future. Possibly some people that you know that I don't."*

"Who are the first couple of names that come to mind right now that you think would take my call to let them know about our homes?" [Wait for response.]

[If they volunteer a name or two, write it down and ask for a way to contact that person or persons. Be sure to note the correct spelling and pronunciation. Get first names so you don't sound like a telemarketer or solicitor when you call them, and get permission to use their name when you contact the other people. If your company offers an incentive for referrals, discuss this inducement for providing names.]

"I'd like to send you our newsletter on a periodic basis just so you will be aware of what we're offering. Is email OK?" [Wait for the response. Confirm their email address or determine which one to use. You can also send them your contact information or vCard and send them a link to your website and blog, if you have one.]

[Discuss your next contact and agree on when and where

that is to be and if it's by email, phone, or in-person. You might set a time to get together for coffee depending on how close your offices are to each other.]

"I'll talk to (see) you again then. Really great hearing from you. Thanks for the call and your help. Goodbye."

LATER WOULD BE BETTER — *"That's fine. It can wait."* [Set up a convenient time to talk again.] *"Talk to you then. Goodbye."*

Call To A Broker Friend

Use this scenario to call and talk with a broker you know very well or well enough to speak to each other and have a conversation when you meet. You want to make sure they know what your current role is and that you want to enlist their help in identifying people that they know that they can bring to your community to look at and purchase a new home from you.

———

"Hi, <first name or nickname of your broker friend>."

"I wanted to make sure that you're aware that I recently began working with <name of your company or community — or both> and we're located at <a general description is probably enough>." [Ask about their recent experiences in the market, and then talk briefly about your homes and what you offer.]

"You know, I could really use your help. Do you have another minute now or would it be better for me to give you a call later?" [Wait for response.]

Now Is OK — *"Fine. Are you working with anyone (Who are you working with) that you could bring by to look at what we have to offer?"* [Wait for response.]

Has a Customer for You — *"That's great. When would it be convenient (When would be a good time) for you to visit?"*

[Set and agree on the time for the visit unless they need check with their customer first — agree on a time to call them to set an appointment.]

"Great, I'll call you <day and time agreed on> (see you <day and time agreed on> at our model). Do you need directions?" [Wait for response and provide directions if needed or agree to email or fax a map — obtain or confirm email address or the fax number to use.]

"Nice talking with you again. Goodbye."

No Customers for You at This Time — *"That's quite all right."*

"I'd like to send you our newsletter periodically just so you will be aware of what we're offering. Is email OK?" [Wait for the response. Confirm their email address or

determine which one to use. You can also send them your contact information or vCard and send them a link to your website and blog, if you have one.]

"Fine. By the way, why don't you visit by yourself so I can show you around?"

Agrees to visit — *"Fine. When's (What's) a good time for you to visit?"* [Set a convenient day and time for the visit.]

"Great, I look forward to showing you our homes. Would you like for me to call or email you a reminder?" [Wait for response.]

Yes — *"Fine. I'll send you a note on <specific day> to remind you of our appointment on <day and time>. Which email address should I use?"* [Confirm the address or write it down as you obtain it.]

"See you then. Goodbye."

No — *"Fine. I'll plan on seeing you then <day and time>. Goodbye."*

Does not want to visit — *"That's fine. If you do meet anyone that you think should know about our community (homes), you can either stop by with them or call for an appointment. Either way, I'll be happy to work with you."*

"I'll call you in a few weeks just to let you know how things are progressing at <name of your community or company> and to see how you're doing."

"I really appreciate your help. Great talking with you again. Goodbye."

LATER WOULD BE BETTER — *"That's fine. It can wait."* [Set up a convenient time to talk again.] *"Talk to you then. Goodbye."*

Call To A New Purchaser

Use this scenario to call and talk with someone who has purchased a new home from you. This can be used anytime after the purchase is firm but *before* the closing. You want to help keep them excited about their decision and request their help in identifying people that they know that you can contact about your new homes.

———

"Hi, <first name or nickname of your homeowner>."

[Thank them again for their purchase, complete your small talk, and then get to the reason for your call.] *"We are really excited about your decision to live here at <name of your community or company> and appreciate you selecting to do business with us. I am sure that you (you guys) are (you're) excited as well about moving into your new home."* [Wait for response.]

"You've probably had a chance to think of several of your friends or associates that you feel should at least look at our homes to see if some of them would want to live here, too." [Wait for response.]

"Who are the first two or three people who come to mind that you think really ought to look at what we have to offer?" [Wait for a response and be prepared to write down any names they give you and ask for a way to contact the friends that they tell you about. Be sure to note the correct spelling and pronunciation. Get first names so you don't sound like a telemarketer or solicitor. Get permission to use your purchaser's name(s) when you contact the other people. If your company offers an incentive program for referrals — maybe just for new purchasers, discuss this with them.]

They Have Names to Give You — *"That's great. I'll invite them to look at what we have to offer, and I'll let you know what happened. Can you think of anyone else?"* [Wait for response.]

"Thanks for your help. I really appreciate it."

"We're really looking forward to having you live here in <name of your community or company> and we appreciate you choosing us to build your new home."

"Please let me know if there's anything I can do for you. Goodbye."

No Names to Give You at This Time — *"That's quite all right. You'll probably think of some later on, and you can tell me about them the next time we talk or you can email them to me. Then I'll invite them to visit us and take a look at our homes."*

"We're really looking forward to having you live here in <name of your community or company> and we appreciate you choosing us to build your new home."

"Please let me know if there's anything I can do for you. Goodbye."

Call To A New Homeowner

Use this scenario to call and talk with someone who has purchased a new home from you and recently moved in. You want to help keep them excited about their decision and request their help in identifying people that they know that you can contact about your new homes.

———

"Hi, <first name or nickname of your homeowner>."

[Thank them again for their purchase, complete your small talk, and then get to the reason for your call.] *"We're really excited about having you live here at <name of your community or company>. I am sure that you (you guys) are (you're) excited as well about living in your new home."* [Wait for response.]

"You've probably had a chance to think of several of your friends or associates that you'd like to show your new home to or feel should at least look at our homes to see if some of them would want to live here, too." [Wait for response.]

"Who are the first two or three people who come to mind that you think really ought to look at what we have to offer?" [Wait for a response and be prepared to write down any names they give you and ask for a way to contact the friends that they tell you about. Be sure to note the correct spelling and pronunciation. Get first names so you don't sound like a telemarketer or solicitor. Get permission to use your purchaser's names when you contact the other people. If your company offers an incentive program for referrals — maybe just for new residents, discuss this with them.]

They Have Names to Give You — *"That's great. I'll invite them to look at what we have to offer, and I'll let you know what happened. Can you think of anyone else?"* [Wait for response.]

"Thanks for your help. I really appreciate it."

"Please let me know if there's anything I can do for you. Goodbye."

No Names to Give You at This Time — *"That's quite all right. You'll probably think of some later on, and you can tell me about them the next time we talk or you can* email them to me. Then I'll invite them to visit us and take a look at our homes."

"We really appreciate you choosing us as your builder and hope that you are adjusting well to your new home."

"Please let me know if there's anything I can do for you. Goodbye."

Alternate Call To A New Purchaser

Use this scenario as another way to talk with someone who has purchased a new home from you — before or immediately after move-in — to ask for their help in identifying people that they know that you can contact about your new homes.

———

"Hi, <first name or nickname of your homeowner>."

[Complete your small talk, and then get to the reason for your call.] "We are really excited about having you live here at <name of your community or company>."

"Since you have selected a home in an area of <name of your community or neighborhood> that still has several available homesites, you might like to help choose some of your new neighbors by having some of your friends live near you. Who are the first three or four names (friends, people) who come to mind that you think you'd *like to have living near you or alongside you in your new neighborhood?"* [Wait for a response.]

[Be prepared to write down any names they give you and ask for a way to contact those people. Be sure to note the correct spelling and pronunciation. Get first names so you don't sound like a telemarketer or solicitor. Get permission to use your purchaser's names when you contact the other people. If your company offers an incentive to customers for referrals, discuss this inducement.]

They Have Names to Give You — *"That's great. I'll invite them to look at what we have to offer, and the next time we talk I'll let you know what happened."*

"Can you think of anyone else?" [Wait for response.]

"Thanks for your help. I really appreciate it."

"Please let me know if there's anything I can do for you. Goodbye."

No Names to Give You at This Time — *"That's quite all right. You'll probably think of some later on, and you can tell me about them the next time we talk or you can email them to me. Then I'll invite them to visit us and take a look at our homes."*

"By the way, let me give you some of my business cards so you'll have them available if you're talking to anyone

that you think should see what we're building or you want to arrange to show them your new home."

"Just have them mention your name when they contact me or let me know who they are so I'll be sure to look out for them." [Continue with your conversation.]

"We really appreciate you choosing us as your builder. Please let me know if there's anything I can do for you. Goodbye."

Call To Existing Homeowners

Use this scenario to call and talk with existing residents of your community that you already have met. They did not purchase a new home from you, but you have spoken to them in the past and developed a relationship with them. You want their help in identifying people that they know that you can contact about your new homes.

———

"Hi, <first name or nickname of your homeowner>." [Complete your small talk, and then get to the reason for your call.]

"We're really glad that you chose to purchase one of our homes and live here in <name of your community or company>. You've probably received many compliments on your home — some from people who might enjoy living here themselves." [Wait for response.]

"I'd like your help for a minute. I imagine you've probably thought of several of your friends or associates that you think should at least look at our homes to see if some of them would want to live here, too." [Wait for response.]

"Who are the first two or three people who come to mind that you think really ought to look at what we have to offer?" [Wait for a response. Be prepared to write down any names they give you and ask for a way to contact them. Be sure to note the correct spelling and pronunciation. Get first names so you don't sound like a telemarketer or solicitor. Get permission to use your homeowner's name(s) when you contact the other people. If your company offers an incentive program for referrals, discuss this with them.]

They Have Names to Give You — *"That's great. I'll invite them to look at what we have to offer, and I'll let you know what happened."*

"Can you think of anyone else?" [Wait for response.] *"Thanks for your help. I really appreciate it."*

"Please let me know if there's anything I can do for you. Goodbye."

No Names to Give You at This Time — *"That's quite all right. You'll probably think of some later on, and you can tell me about them the next time we talk or you can* *email them to me. Then I'll invite them to visit us and take a look at our homes."*

"Please let me know if there's anything I can do for you. Goodbye."

Call Back To Your Regular Service & Repair People

Use this scenario to call and talk with people that you see on a regular basis who provide technical and repair services and help maintain your office and equipment. This would be a call between their regular visits — after you talked with them and made the request for help in person and they said to check back with them. You want their help in identifying people that they know that you can contact about your new homes.

———

"Hi, <first name or nickname of your service provider>."

[Complete your small talk, and then get to the reason for your call.] *"When we spoke the last time you were here, I asked you who you might know or might have heard of in your travels who is in the market for a different home that should take a look at what we have to offer, and you told me that you needed some time to think of someone. I was wondering who you have thought of that should take a look at our homes?"* [Wait for response.]

[If he or she readily volunteers a name or two now, write it down and ask for a way to contact them. Be sure to note the correct spelling and pronunciation. Get first names so you don't sound like a telemarketer or solicitor, and get permission to use the person's name that is giving you the referrals when you contact the other people.]

They Have Names to Give You — *"That's great. I will call them and invite them to take a look at what we offer here at <name of your community or company>. The next time you drop by I'll let you know what happened."*

"Can you think of anyone else?" [Wait for response.]

"Thanks. I appreciate your help. See you next time (or specific day if it's soon). Have a great day."

"By the way, have you passed out any of the business cards I gave you?" [Wait for response and discuss the circumstances if that if it has happened.]

"Thanks again. Goodbye."

No Names to Give You at This Time — *"That's quite all right. Thanks for trying."*

"Again, if anyone comes to mind that you think should know about our community (homes), you can tell them

about what we're doing, or you can let me know who they are whenever you come in and I'll invite them to come and take a look."

"I really appreciate your help. See you again next time. By the way, have you passed out any of the business cards I gave you?" [Wait for response and discuss the circumstances if that if it has happened.]

"Have a good one. Goodbye."

Call Back To Your
Building Professionals

Use this scenario to call and talk with the professionals that are involved with creating and marketing your new homes. This would be a call between visits. You want their help in identifying people that they know that you can contact about your new homes.

———

"Hi, <first name or nickname of your professional>."

[Complete your small talk, and then get to the reason for your call.] *"When we spoke the last time you were here, I asked you who you might know or might have heard of in your travels who is in the market for a different home that should take a look at what we have to offer, and you asked me to call you (told me that you needed some time to think of someone). I was wondering who you have thought of that should take a look at our homes?"* [Wait for response.]

[If he or she readily volunteers a name or two now, write it down and ask for a way to contact them. Be sure to note the correct spelling and pronunciation. Get first names so you don't sound like a telemarketer or solicitor, and get permission to use the person's name that is giving you the referrals when you contact the other people.]

They Have Names to Give You — *"That's great. I will call them and invite them to take a look at what we offer here at <name of your community or company>. The next time you drop by I'll let you know what happened."*

"Can you think of anyone else?" [Wait for response.]

"Thanks. I appreciate your help. See you next time. Have a great day."

"By the way, have you passed out any of the business cards I gave you?" [Wait for response and discuss the circumstances if that if it has happened.]

"Thanks again. Goodbye."

No Names to Give You at This Time — *"That's quite all right. Thanks for trying."*

"Again, if anyone comes to mind that you think should know about our community (homes), you can tell them about what we're doing, or you can let me know who they are whenever you come in and I'll invite them to come and take a look. I really appreciate your help."

"See you again next time. By the way, have you passed out any of the business cards I gave you?" [Wait for response and discuss the circumstances if that if it has happened.]

"Have a good one. Goodbye."

Asking For A Referral On An Incoming Phone Inquiry

Use this scenario after talking with someone who called in for information about your homes when you learn that they do not appear to like or want what you have to offer — ask for their help in identifying other people who might be interested in a new home.

———

"I appreciate your call and I am sorry that you don't think we can meet your needs from what we've just briefly discussed, but I'm just curious. You must have thought we were worth checking out or you wouldn't have called, so let me ask you this."

"Who can you think of who might be in a similar

situation as you that you think might like to look at what we have to offer? I'd be happy to contact them and see if they would be interested in what we have to offer here at <name of your community or company — or both>." [Wait for response.]

[If they volunteer a name or two, write it down and ask for a way to contact that person or persons. Be sure to note the correct spelling and pronunciation. Get first names so you don't sound like a telemarketer or solicitor, and get permission to use the person's name that is giving you the referrals when you contact the names they are giving you. Determine the best form of contact for the people who are being referred to you.]

They Have Names to Give You — *"That's great. Can you think of anyone else?"* [Wait for response.] *"Thanks for your help. I really appreciate it. Goodbye."*

No Names to Give You at This Time — *"That's quite all right. Thanks for trying and thanks for your interest in <name of your community or company>. Goodbye."*

Post-Visit Call To Ask For A Referral

Use this scenario as a post-visit phone call to someone after an initial presentation in your model center — as part of a scheduled or planned contact or as a special call just to ask for their help in identifying other people who might be interested in a new home.

"Hello <use their first name — or their nickname if they provided one when you met them>? This is <your name> from <name of your community or company — or both>."

"I really enjoyed getting to meet you and being able to tell you a little bit about who we are and what we are going to be doing at <name of your community> (in our community, homes)."

"I think you'd agree that until you experience what we're here doing firsthand, it's kind of hard to fully appreciate what we're offering."

"Now that you've had a chance to see what we're all about, maybe you've thought of some people who ought to see for themselves what we offer. Who are the first two names that come to mind that I should call or email to let them know about our homes?" [Wait for response.]

[Be prepared to write down any names they give you and ask for a way to contact those people. Be sure to note the correct spelling and pronunciation. Get first names so you don't sound like a telemarketer or solicitor. Get permission to use your resident's names when you contact the other people. If your company offers an incentive to customers for referrals, discuss this inducement for providing names.]

They Have Names to Give You — *"That's great. I'll contact them and let you know what they said. Can you think of anyone else?"* [Wait for response.]

"Thanks for your help. I really appreciate it. Goodbye."

No Names to Give You at This Time — *"That's quite all right. Thanks for trying. Maybe the name of someone will come to you later that you can pass along to me."*

"I'd like to send you our newsletter periodically just so you will be aware of what we're offering. Is email OK?" [Wait for the response. Confirm their email address or determine which one to use. You can also talk about or send them a link to your blog if you have one.]

"Fine. I'll call you again in a month or so just to let you know how things are progressing here at <name of your community or company>. I'll also want to make sure that you have received what I have sent you."

"If you happen to think of anyone between now and when we talk again who might be interested in the opportunities we offer here at <name of your community or company>, you can tell me about them at that time."

"Again, thanks for your help (interest). Good-bye."

Post-Visit Call To Ask For Additional Referrals

Use this scenario as another reason to call someone that you've talked with about your homes after they already gave you the name of someone that you could contact during your initial meeting or previous telephone conversation with them — this time to thank them and pursue additional referrals.

––––––

"Hello <use their first name — or a nickname if they indicated one when you met them>? This is <your name> from <name of your community or company — or both>."

"When we met (spoke) the other day (a specific day), you gave me the name of <state the name or names of the people who were provided> as being in the market for a new home and possibly interested in what we have to offer here at <your community or company — or both>."

"I really appreciate you sharing their name (these names) with me, and I wanted to let you know that I called them and <report generally on your results>."

"I was wondering if you had been able to think of any other people who might be able to consider the new homes that we offer here at <name of your community or company>" [Wait for response.]

They Have More Names to Give You — *"Great. Who are they?"* [Wait for response.]

[Be prepared to write down any names they give you and ask for a way to contact those people. Be sure to note the correct spelling and pronunciation. Get first names so you don't sound like a telemarketer or solicitor. Get permission to use their name(s) when you contact the other people.]

"I'll contact these people just as I did the others that you gave to me and I will call you back to let you know what happens. Thanks again for your help. Goodbye."

No Names to Give You at This Time — *"That's quite all right. I appreciate your help."*

"By the way, I'd like to take you to breakfast next week (whenever our schedules allow within the next couple of weeks) to show my appreciation for your help." [Wait for response and agree upon a day, time, and location if they accept your invitation.]

"Would you like for me to call you or email you a reminder?" [Wait for response.]

  Yes — *"Fine. I'll send you a note on <mention the specific day> to remind you of our appointment on <day, time, and location>. Which email address should I use?"* [Confirm the address or write it down as you obtain it.]

  "I look forward to seeing you then. Goodbye."

  No — *"Fine. I'll plan on seeing you then on <mention the day and time> at <place>. Goodbye."*

Second Call To Ask For A Referral

Use this scenario to call someone you talked with about your homes previously but they were unable to provide you with any referrals to contact during your initial meeting or your last telephone conversation with them — this time to ask them again for any names they can furnish.

———

"Hello <preferably use their first name — even use their nickname if they indicated one>? This is <your name> from <name of your community or company — or both>."

"When we met (spoke) the other day (a specific day), I asked who you knew that might be interested in what we build here, and you weren't able to think of anyone. I thought that maybe since then that maybe you'd thought of one or two people that should know about what we are offering."

"Who comes to mind now that I should call (email) to have them take a look at what we offer here at <name of your community or company>?" [Wait for response.]

No Names to Give You at This Time — *"I understand, and I appreciate your time to talk with me again."*

"I'd like to send you our newsletter on a periodic basis just so you'll be aware of what we're offering. Is email OK?" [Wait for response. Confirm their email address or

determine which one to use. You can also talk about or send them a link to your blog if you have one.]

"I'll check back with you in a few weeks to make sure you're getting the newsletter, and if anyone comes to mind that you think should know about our homes (community), you can tell me then. Goodbye."

They Have Names to Give You — *"Great. Who are they?"* [Wait for response. Write down any names they give you and ask for a way to contact those people. Be sure to note the correct spelling and pronunciation. Get first names so you don't sound like a telemarketer or solicitor. Get permission to use their name when you contact the other people.]

"I'll call them and invite them to take a look at what we offer here at <name of your community or company>. Then I'll call you after I have spoken with them to let you know what happened."

"Thanks for your help. I really appreciate it. Good-bye."

Leaving A Voice Message After A Brief Initial Meeting

Use this scenario when you get the person's voice mail when you call. Be prepared to leave a voice mail message, but only leave the following message — and only do it on the initial call. After that, no messages regardless of how many times you call and reach the machine. Just hang up before the tone.

———

"Hi, <their first name>. This is <your complete name, first and last> of <your company or community — or both>."

"I met you briefly last night (the other day, Tuesday, last Wednesday, over the weekend) at (mention the specific event or place where you met, such as Chamber of Commerce breakfast, church, jury duty, Little League game, the mall, a specific store or restaurant, the Rotary Club, PTA, etc.) — basically just long enough for us to exchange business cards." [Be sure to mention the place or the circumstances for the meeting.]

"I was calling to say hello again and see if we could set up a time to talk for a few minutes over coffee to learn more about each other's business. I possibly could use your help."

"I'm sorry I missed you. I'll try again another time, but my number here is <telephone number>."

"Thanks. I look forward to talking with you again soon."

[If they call back, that's great. Be prepared to have a conversation with them just as if you had reached them successfully when you telephoned originally.]

Leaving A Message With An Assistant

Use this scenario when someone other than the person you are calling answers the phone, or the person you are attempting to call is not available. Be prepared to leave a message with their assistant or whoever volunteers to take a message, but only leave the following message — and only do this on the initial call. It's not necessary that you leave a message, but if you choose to do so, be careful not to leave too many details because you don't want the assistant or the "screener" to try to help you or to tell you that the person who are calling would not be interested in helping you.

———

[Begin this way when someone other than the person you are calling answers.] *"Hi, is <use their first name> in today (available)? This is <your name, first and last>."*

[Act like you are old friends — and only mention your company name if specifically requested.]

[If you decide to leave a message rather than just saying that you'll call back without providing any other information, you can go ahead with the following.] *"I met him (her) briefly last night (the other day, Tuesday, last Wednesday, over the weekend) at (mention the specific event or place where you met, such as Chamber of Commerce breakfast, church, Little League game, jury duty, the mall, a specific store or restaurant, the*

Rotary Club, PTA, etc.). I was calling to continue our conversation."

"I'll try again another time. Thank you." [Don't volunteer your phone number. Provide it you choose to if you are asked for it, but it's not necessary. Just say that you'll call back later.]

[OR]

[For someone you know fairly well] *"He/she knows who I am, and I'll call back another time."*

[You may try calling again, but do not leave a second message — just your name.]

6

Reaching Out In Writing

The Value Of Writing

In addition to using personal and telephone communication with people that you already know, sometimes it might be easier or more convenient to reach out to them with a letter, email, or text message.

It isn't always quicker or as effective as talking to someone in person or by telephone, but you can do it according to your schedule and not be concerned whether the person you are connecting with is available at that particular moment to receive your message.

Using a written message, such as email, card, or letter — not text or instant messaging — is also useful for documenting your requests and for passing along your contact information.

When you need to include a postcard, your business card, or a survey, written communication is the best form of contact to use.

Letters work well also when it's been a long time since you have talked to your friend or customer. They help re-establish your relationship. Then you can follow with a phone call or email.

Using Email

While email is not appropriate for working with people that you don't know because it's less formal and their spam filter may not allow your message to get through, it's fine to use emails for communicating with friends and others that you know.

When you send emails, your email address and your company website address (URL) should be **active links** so that the person you're contacting can reply back or go to your website without entering any information.

They can just hit the link ("'control' + 'click'") and go right to a reply screen with your email address already filled in, or they can go directly to your website homepage.

Also, go for a consistent look in your email address. Don't use yourname@gmail.com address part of the time and yourname@yourcompany.com at other times.

Even though you are communicating with friends, do not use a personal-looking email address unless you are such good friends that they will easily recognize it.

Most of the time, addresses such as "fredlikesfishing@," "packersfan@," or "mary1267@" are too casual for business communication.

If you don't have an email at your community or corporate domain name — or choose not to use it since your friends may not recognize it — go with a gmail or yahoo email address.

Getting Email Delivered

You want the person who receives your email message to open it and read it, so avoid anything that might keep it from getting into their inbox.

If you're not sure how their email client accepts attachments, it's best not to include them and to put them in the body of your email. Keep them very short.

People worry about viruses, and some email programs could reject or your message, or send it to the junk folder.

In your subject line, avoid anything cutesy or vague. Putting the name of your community or anything to do with new homes may get flagged. Just include your own name, such as *"Message from Steve Hoffacker."*

Familiarity Helps

Unlike contacting strangers where a certain amount of formality and propriety are important, connecting with your friends and people you know can be more casual and spontaneous.

Messages can be brief and can include more personal references. You can ask about them and their family or recall a common activity, for instance.

Don't be sloppy — you are still conducting business. However, phrases, some slang, and even humor can be used to help it sound more conversational with your friends. Avoid anything off-color.

Email is never advisable for an initial introduction to someone you are attempting to establish a relationship with but is fine to use with people you know. Just make sure you have a current email address before reaching out to them.

Texting And Instant Messaging

Text messaging ("texting") may be a good way to contact some of your closest friends and relatives — especially if you have texted them previously about others matters or know that they like to communicate this way. Perhaps they have texted you previously. It can be a good change of pace for contact.

Nevertheless, texting should never be done to introduce yourself to someone you have not met and should only be used when you know the person well enough for them to appreciate that you contacted them in this way and for them to respond to your text.

Even social networking sites like Facebook and Twitter can be great resources for leaving messages and communicating with your friends and network.

Using "chat" on Facebook or instant messaging on other sites — when you notice friends and acquaintances online — is an excellent way to initiate or maintain contact with them.

Writing Requires Minimal Effort

In this chapter, I've assembled just a few examples of letters, cards, and emails (and a couple of text messages) that you can use as you contact friends, people that you do business with, those you have met socially or at business functions, ones you see occasionally, friends that you see often or rarely, people you have sold homes to or talked with during a presentation, professionals whose services you use, or others that you want to communicate with in writing about what you are doing and how you can use their help.

Remember the reason you use the letter, card, or email is to communicate when a personal approach is not practical or necessary. Having your message delivered must happen before it can be read.

Use these suggested letters, cards and emails exactly as they are or modify them for your writing style, personality, and degree of formality.

Intentionally, the suggested letters are a little more formal, printed cards a little so, and notecards fairly short and informal since they are handwritten. The suggested emails are in a relatively informal email style with more paragraphs than a letter.

Writing Is Only One Approach

Remember that the reason you are using the letter, card, email, or even in a few cases a text message, is to communicate to people you already know when you do not need actually to be speaking directly to them by phone or in-person — or when reaching them by phone or seeing them in-person is not easily done.

In some cases, this approach might be sufficient. In others, this will be a prelude to a phone conversation or meeting.

Use these suggested letters, cards, and email exactly as they are or modify them for your writing style.

They should not have a strong sales message.

The main thing your communication is doing is requesting help from your circle of contacts.

Your Signature Block

In the interest of keeping the following examples of letters as short as possible — showing just the salutation and main body of the letter — the following information (even if you already have mentioned it elsewhere in the body of the letter, such as your phone number, email address, or website) should be added after the text provided as a way of closing the letter:

> *Sincerely,*
>   [space]
> *<Community or company name — or both >*
>   [space]
> *<Your signature> (digital for emails)*
>   [space]
> *<Your name — as you want your customers to call you — plus any professional designations>*
> *<Your position or title>*
> *<Your direct phone line or extension>*
> *<Your fax number>*
> *<Your cell phone number>*
> *<Your email address> (linked in emails)*
> *<Your company website> (linked in emails)*
> *<Your company blog address> (linked in emails)*
>   [space]
> *<Your community or company "tagline">*

[space]
<Your social media widgets> (linked in emails)
[space]
<Any attachments or enclosures>

Signing Cards

For notecards and postcards — especially ones that are handwritten or commercial greeting cards — just sign them in your own hand. Don't use a stamp or electronic signature

Using just your first name is fine — especially if you know them very well. For others that you know but aren't sure if they will recognize you by just your first name because they likely know several people with your same first name or you haven't talked with in a while, you might want to use your complete name.

You don't need to sign your name with your professional designations or title. That will be on your business card that you are enclosing.

Be sure to enclose a business card in the envelope along with the note or place it inside the greeting card (obviously this can't be done with a postcard) to supply the other contact information — even if some of your contact information is printed elsewhere on the card.

For emails, include hot (active) links to your email

address, website, blog, social media profiles, and any references that you include.

The Inside Address

Unlike a letter to someone that you haven't met before, most of your letters to your circle of contacts will be less formal. As such, they won't require an inside address.

When you are sending a letter to someone you just met as the first step in developing the relationship, you may want to use a customary inside address with:

*<Name, including any professional designations> or
<Names, if a couple>
<Title or Position, if applicable>
<Name of Business, if sent to the business>
<Business Address, including department, suite number, floor, or building, if sent to the business>
<Home Address, including apartment number, if sent to the residence>
<City, State, Zip>*

For notes, cards, emails, and text messages — and for the majority or your letters — the inside address would not be used.

It's a good idea to put the date at the top of any letter, card, or note that you are sending — even if there is no inside address.

Letter After A Brief Introduction

Use this letter — typically written on your computer and printed out although it can be handwritten if you like — after meeting someone briefly at a business or social function to acknowledge the meeting and set up a future telephone conversation with them. At that future meeting, you can enlist their help and pursue a business relationship with them. Keep this letter fairly brief and cordial — no sales message.

———

<First name of new friend or acquaintance>,

I'm glad I had the opportunity (chance) to meet you last night (Tuesday, yesterday, recently) at <specific event or place where you met, such as seminar, mixer, reception, Chamber of Commerce breakfast, church, Little League game, youth soccer game, seminar, Rotary Club, etc.>. Unfortunately, we didn't get a chance to talk to each other very much. It seemed like we just met long enough to exchange business cards and that was about it.

I would like to learn more about your business and get a chance, as well, to tell you about what we are doing here at <name of your community or company>. I will give you a call in a couple of days to see when you are available to grab a cup of coffee so we can talk some more.

In the meantime, you may reach me at <telephone number> or email me at <email address>. You might also want to visit our website at <website address>.

I look forward to talking with you again.

Printed Notecard After
A Brief Introduction

Rather than a letter (handwritten or printed), you may choose to use a notecard, such a one imprinted with the name and logo of your company or community that you can print out with your message on your computer. Use this after meeting someone briefly at a business or social function to acknowledge the meeting and set up a future telephone conversation. At that future meeting, you can enlist their help and pursue a business relationship with them. Notes are typically brief and to the point — avoid a sales message or reference.

———

<First name of new friend or acquaintance>,

I'm glad I had the opportunity (chance) to meet you last night (Tuesday, yesterday, last week) at <specific event or place where you met, such as seminar, mixer, reception, charity event, golf outing, home builders or real estate association event, Chamber of Commerce breakfast, church, Little League game, youth soccer game, Rotary Club, committee meeting, etc.>.

I will give you a call in a couple of days to see when you are available for coffee so we can talk some more.

In the meantime, you may reach me at <telephone number> or email me at <email address>.

You might also want to visit our website at <website address>.

I look forward to talking with you again.

Handwritten Notecard After
A Brief Introduction

You may want to use a handwritten note on your company notecards rather than a computer printed message to contact someone you just met at a business or social function to set up a future telephone conversation. Just write as legibly as you can. You may want to print in all caps if your penmanship is not strong. At that future meeting, you can enlist their help and pursue a business relationship with them. You want your note to be cordial and fairly brief.

––––––

<First name of new friend or acquaintance>,

I'm glad we met last night (Tuesday, yesterday, last week) at <the name or type of the event or place where you met, such as seminar, mixer, reception, charity event, golf

outing, home builder association or broker events, Chamber of Commerce breakfast, church, Little League game, youth soccer game, Rotary Club, committee meeting, etc.>.

I will give you a call in a couple of days to see when you are available for coffee so we can talk some more.

In the meantime, you may reach me at <telephone number> or email me at <email address>.

You might also want to visit our website at <website address>.

I look forward to talking with you again.

Handwritten Note In A Greeting Card After A Brief Introduction

You can choose to use a handwritten message inside a commercial greeting card (a card with a success message or one with an inspirational picture and message) rather than using a note or letter — just jot your message in the blank space above the fold or on the left side of the fold of the card to contact someone you just met at a business or social function to set up a future telephone conversation. At that future meeting, you can enlist their help and pursue a business relationship with them. You want your note to be cordial and very brief.

<First name of new friend or acquaintance>,

I'm glad we met last night (Tuesday, yesterday, last week) at <name or type of the specific event or place where you met, such as seminar, mixer, reception, charity event, golf outing, home builder association or broker event, Chamber breakfast, church, Little League game, youth soccer game, Rotary Club, committee meeting, etc.>.

I will give you a call in a couple of days to see when you are available for coffee so we can talk some more.

I enclosed my card with my contact information.

I look forward to talking with you again.

Email After A Brief Introduction

Email is a very acceptable and convenient way for businesspeople and friends to communicate today, so you may choose to use this rather than a letter, note, or card to contact someone you just met at a business or social function to set up a future telephone conversation. At that future meeting, you can enlist their help and pursue a business relationship with them. This is a fairly informal method of contact and should be used within 24 hours of the original meeting.

———

<First name of new friend or acquaintance>,
I'm glad I had the opportunity (chance) to meet you (I enjoyed meeting you) last night (this morning, yesterday, over the weekend, Wednesday morning, Monday night) at <specific event or place where you met, such as seminar, mixer, reception, Chamber of Commerce breakfast, church, Little League game, youth soccer game, the mall, a specific store or restaurant, Rotary Club, etc.>.

I would like to learn more about your business and what you do. I'd also like to tell you a little about (talk about) what we are doing here at <name of your community or company — or both>.

I'll give you a call in a couple of days to see when you are available to get (have, let me buy you) a cup of coffee.

If you like, you can contact me at <telephone number> or <email address> [linked].

You might also want to check out (take a look at, visit) our website at <website address> [linked].

I look forward to talking with you again.

Letter To Friend Or Acquaintance

Use this letter on your company or community letterhead to notify friends and acquaintances of your new position and to lay the foundation for referrals. This is going to be a more casual and informal style of letter than most you would use. Keep it relatively short since you can visit with them later or use text, phone, or email to pursue your referral needs. Keep this letter strictly informational, as you don't want to appear that the only reason you are contacting them is for their help.

———

<First name of your friend or acquaintance>,

I don't know if you've heard or not, but I wanted to make sure you knew (are aware) that I am now representing <your community or company — or both>, located at <physical address>.

I'm excited about the opportunities here. This is a great company, and we are developing a community (neighborhood) of <number of homes> of <affordable townhomes, luxury single family homes, low-maintenance coach homes, etc.>.

For now, I just wanted to make sure you were aware of what I'm doing and that you have my current contact information.

I'll call you soon to see (discuss, talk about) when we can get together (have coffee, get a drink, grab lunch, have breakfast).
In the meantime, feel free to call me anytime on my cell phone at <number> or email me at <email address>.

Printed Notecard To A
Friend Or Acquaintance

Rather than a letter, you may choose to use an informal note or notecard card imprinted with the name and logo of your company or community that you print out on your computer to notify friends and acquaintances of your new position and to lay the foundation for referrals. The note format is good because you want to keep it relatively short anyway since you can visit with them later or text, phone, or email them to pursue your referral needs. Keep this note strictly informational — you don't want it to appear that you are contacting them just for their help.

———

<First name of your friend or acquaintance>,

I wanted to make sure you are aware (know) that I just started representing <name of your community or company — or both> located at <physical address>. (I've changed companies since we last spoke, and now I'm <title of position> here at <name of your community or company — or both> in <name of area or physical location>.)

I just started (I've been here just <approximate length of time>).

I'll call you soon to give you some more details and see when we can get together for a cup of coffee (breakfast, lunch).

For now, I just wanted to make sure you were aware of what I'm doing and that you have my current contact information.

In the meantime, feel free to call me anytime on my cell phone at <number> or email me at <email address>.

Handwritten Notecard To A Friend Or Acquaintance

Use this personal handwritten notecard on your official company or community notepaper or notecard to notify your friends and acquaintances of your current status and to lay the foundation for referrals. Keep this note strictly informational, as you don't want to appear that you are contacting them just for their help. You may want to print in all caps rather than use cursive.

———

<First name of your friend or acquaintance>,

I wanted to make sure that you're aware that I just started representing <name of your community or company — or both> located at <physical address>.

I've just been here <approximate length of time>.
I'll call you soon to give you some more details and see when we can get together for a cup of coffee (breakfast, lunch, a drink).

I just wanted to make sure you were aware of what I'm doing and that you have my current contact information.

Email To A Friend Or Acquaintance
On Your New Position

Email is a convenient way to communicate with friends and acquaintances as long as you have their current email address. This informal message is a great way to let people know what you are doing and to lay the foundation for referrals. This note should remain primarily informational, but there can be some personal references in it because of the format. Just don't make it seem that you are contacting them just for their help.

———

<First name of your friend or acquaintance>,

Just a quick note to let you know that I've relocated (moved) from my last position. I wasn't sure if you knew about this so I wanted to make sure I told you that I recently started here as <title of position> at <name of your community/company>, located at <physical address or landmark>.

I've attached a vCard with my new contact information. I'm excited about the opportunities here. We are a community (neighborhood) of <number of homes> of <affordable townhomes, luxury single family homes, low-maintenance coach homes, etc.>.

I'll call you soon to see (discuss/talk about) when we can get together.

In the meantime, feel free to give me a call on my cell at <cell number> or email me at <email address> [linked].

Talk to you soon.

Email To A Friend Or Acquaintance For A Referral

After you have re-established contact with your close circle of contacts, email is a great way to reach out to them to request the names of people for you to contact that might be interested in a new home.

———

<First name of your friend or acquaintance>,

When we last spoke (talked) I told you about what we are doing here at <name of your community/company>, and I mentioned that I could use your help in identifying people that might be looking for a new home such as we offer.
Has anyone come to mind that I could talk to?

I just want them to see for themselves if what we offer interests them. If it does, great. If not, that's OK, too.

Let me know who I should be talking to, and then let them know that I will contacting them.

Thanks for your help.

Text To A Friend, Relative, Or Acquaintance For Update

Use this brief text message to contact someone you know well enough to communicate with them in this way (relative, close friend, or acquaintance) to let them know of your new position and to set up another contact by phone or have an email or text mail exchange with them. For purposes of this template, abbreviations that often are used in texting will not be used. However, if you have already been texting this person and typically type all in lower case or use shorthand or abbreviations, then using "4" for "for," "cn u" for "can you," "ur" for "your," "BTW" for "by the way" and other such notations or styling would be fine to use. Otherwise, avoid them and keep it businesslike.

<Their first name>, I just started selling homes here at <name of your company/builder> in <general location>. Would love to catch up with you over coffee. What's your schedule (convenient for you)? <Your first name>

Text To A Friend, Relative, Or Acquaintance For Referral

Use this brief text message to contact someone you know well enough to communicate with them in this way (relative, friend, or acquaintance). You want to find out who they know that might have an interest in buying a new home that they can refer to you. Again, if you have already been texting this person and typically use shorthand notations, it's fine to continue doing that. Otherwise, keep it businesslike.

<Their first name>, I can use your help. I think I told you that I am selling new homes in <name of your area> with <name of your company or builder>. I would appreciate hearing about anyone that you know who might be looking for a new home in my area in the <price range>. Any ideas? Thanks. <Your first name>

Email To A Social Networking Contact

Use this email message to contact any person that you know through social networking sites that you have blogged with or connected with online. You mainly want to talk with them by phone or have an email exchange — rather than set a meeting — to determine who they know who has an interest in buying a new home and who they can refer to you.

———

<Their first name>,

[If you're contacting them through the social networking site and using the email platform there, there won't be a need for establishing how you know each other. Otherwise, an opening line reminding them of how you know each other might be necessary.]

In case you weren't aware of what I do, I sell new homes in <name of your area or town> with <name of your company or builder>.

We are a neighborhood of <number of homes> of <affordable townhomes, luxury single family homes, low-maintenance coach homes, etc.> and offer <architectural style or design of homes> priced from <price range>.

I thought maybe you could help me. I am looking for people who might be interested in a new home in my area — now or in the near future.

If you have any ideas for anyone in my market or anyone who might be relocating here, I would appreciate hearing about them.

If you can't think of anyone, that's OK. Maybe later. Thanks for your help.

Email To A Broker Friend

Email is a convenient way to reach out to brokers that you know to let them know about your new position and to request referrals. Because you both are interested in possibly making a sale at your community, you can go ahead and ask for a referral on the initial contact with your friend.

———

<First name of your broker friend or acquaintance>,

Just a quick note to let you know that I've relocated (moved) from my last position. I wasn't sure if you knew about this so I wanted to make sure I told you that I recently started here as <title of position> at <name of your community/company>, located at <physical address or landmark>.

I'm excited about the opportunities here. We are a community (neighborhood) of <number of homes> of

<affordable townhomes, luxury single family homes, low-maintenance coach homes, etc.> in the <price range>.

If you're currently working with or know of anyone whom you think might like to see what we offer, I would love to be to show you and them what we have to offer here and get your thoughts on it.
I'll give you a call soon to talk more about what we have and how it might work out for some of your customers.

In the meantime, feel free to give me a call on my cell at <cell number> or email me at <email address> [linked]. I've attached a vCard with my new contact information.

Talk to you soon.

Letter To A New Purchaser

Use this letter that you generate on your computer to contact someone who has purchased a new home from you but has not closed on it or moved into it yet. Your letter welcomes them to your community and requests their help in identifying people who should know about your homes.

———

<First name or names of your new purchaser>,

Welcome again to our <name of your community> family. We are looking forward to having you as one of our new residents.

As you are getting ready to move into your new home, you probably have had several friends, family members, and co-workers ask about your new home and show an interest in what you have selected.
I would love to talk with (show) anyone that you think should know about our homes how they could live here at <name of your community>, too.

I have enclosed a stamped, addressed postcard for you to jot down the names and contact information for a couple of people that have said they would like to live here or ones that you think need to hear (see) what we're all about. If you prefer, you can email it to me at <email address>.

Thanks for your help. If there's anything I can do for you, please let me know. It won't be much longer until you're ready to move in.

Printed Notecard To A New Purchaser

Rather than a letter, you may choose to use a notecard imprinted with the name and logo of your company or community that you print out on your computer to contact a new purchaser. It's less formal than a letter.

This note is used to welcome them to your community and ask for referrals.

———

<First name or names of your new purchaser>,

Welcome again to our <name of your community> family. We are looking forward to having live here.
As you are getting ready to move into your new home, you probably have had several friends, family members, and co-workers ask about your new home and show an interest in what you have selected.

I would love to talk with (meet) some of them and show them how they could live here at <name of your community>, too.

I have enclosed a stamped, addressed postcard for you to jot down the names and contact information for a couple of people that have said they would like to live here or ones that you think need to hear (see) what we're all about.

If you prefer, you can email the information to me at <email address>.

Thanks for your help. If there's anything I can do for you as you are getting ready to move-in, please let me know.

Handwritten Notecard

To A New Purchaser

Instead of mailing something "typed," you may want to use something much less formal such as a handwritten notecard imprinted with your community or company name or logo and basic contact information on it to welcome a new purchaser and ask for a referral.

———

<First name or names of your new purchaser>,

As you are preparing to move into your new home here at <name of community, neighborhood name within the community, or their actual street address if not part of a specifically named area>, we again want to welcome you to our family and thank you for selecting us to build your new home.

I have enjoyed getting to know you, and I could use your help in identifying some of your friends that you think should know about us.

I have enclosed a stamped, addressed postcard so you can let me know about anyone that you think should experience what we offer. If you prefer, you can email the information to me at <email address>.

Thanks for your help. If there's anything I can do for you, please let me know.

Email To A New Purchaser

<First name of your new purchaser>,

Welcome again to our <name of your community> family. We are looking forward to having live here soon.

As you are getting ready to move into your new home, you probably have had several friends, family members, and co-workers ask about your new home and show an interest in what you have selected.

I would love to talk (meet) with them and show them (talk about) how they could live here at <your community>, too.

Just hit the "reply" button above and send me the names and contact information for a couple of people that have said they would like to live here or ones that you think need to hear (see) what we're all about.

Thanks for your help. If there's anything I can do for you as you getting ready to move-in, please let me know.

Letter To A New Resident

Use this computer-generated letter on your company or community letterhead to contact someone who has just moved into a new home they purchased from you. Your letter welcomes them to your community (again) and requests their help in identifying people who should know about your homes.

———

<First name or names of your new purchaser>,

Let me welcome you officially to our community.

We're glad you're here living in your new home.
As you have been moving in and getting settled in your new home, I'm sure you've had several friends and family members stop by to see you and visit your new home.

I'd love to meet and talk with some of them and show them how they could enjoy living here at <name of your community>, too.

I have enclosed a stamped, addressed postcard for you to jot down the names and contact information for a couple of people that have expressed an interest in our homes so that I can contact them. If you prefer, you can email it to me at <email address> or drop by the office.

Thanks again for your help. If there's anything I can do for you, please let me know.

Printed Notecard To
A New Resident

Rather than a letter, you may choose to contact a new resident with a notecard imprinted with the name and logo of your company or community that you print out on your computer. It's less formal than a letter. This note is used to welcome them to your community (again) and ask for referrals.

———

<First name or names of your new resident>,
Welcome again to our <name of your community> family. I'm sure you're happy to finally be moved in, and we're excited to have you living here now.

As you have been moving in and getting settled in your new home, I imagine you've had several friends and family members stop by to see your new home and wish you well.

I'd love to meet and talk with some of them about how they could enjoy living here at <name of your community>, too.

Just email their contact information to me at <email address> or drop it by the office.

Thanks again for your help.

If there's anything I can do for you as you are getting adjusted to your new home, please let me know.

Handwritten Notecard
To A New Resident

Instead of mailing something "typed," you may want to use an informal handwritten notecard to welcome a new resident and ask for a referral.

————

<First name or names of your new resident>,
Welcome again to <name of your community>. How does it feel to actually be moved in?

I'm sure you've been receiving many compliments on your new home from friends (friends and relatives, friends and family), and I'd love to meet some of them to talk with them about living here at <name of your community>, too.

Please use the enclosed postcard to let me know about anyone that you think should experience what we offer.

If you prefer, you can email the information to me at <email address> or drop it off at the office.

Thanks for your help. If there's anything I can do for you as you're getting settled, please let me know.

Handwritten Greeting Card
Note To A New Resident

Rather than anything "typed," or even a handwritten notecard, you may choose to use a commercial greeting card with a "Congratulations" or "Welcome" cover and inside message. Keep the note short and on the blank space opposite the printed message. Use this to officially welcome a new resident and to request referrals.

———

<First name of new friend or acquaintance>,
Welcome again to <name of your community>. Now it's official.

As you are getting settled in your new home, I'd really appreciate it if you could let me know about anyone that you think should experience what we offer. Be thinking of who that might be and then you can let me know the next time we talk.

Thanks for your help. If there's anything I can do for you, please let me know.

Email To A New Resident

Use this less formal email message for a more immediate way to welcome a new resident to their new home and your community and also to request their help in furnishing a referral.

———

<First name or names of your new purchaser>,

Welcome again to <name of your community>, and welcome officially into your new home. We are excited to have you living here.

As you have been moving in and getting settled in your new home, I imagine that you've have had several friends and family members stop by and compliment you on your new home.
I'd love to meet and talk with some of your friends about how they could enjoy living here at <name of your community> also.

Just hit the "reply" button above and send me the names and contact information for a couple of people that have said they would like to live here or ones that you think need to hear (see) what we're all about.

I'll let you know when they plan on visiting and bring them by to see you when they visit.

Thanks for your help. If there's anything I can do for you, please let me know.

Letter To An Established Resident

Use this typed or computer printed letter to contact someone who lives in your community that you already have met that bought their new home from someone in your company other than you. Your letter should again thank them for doing business with your company and then request their help in identifying people who should know about your homes.

———

<First name or names of your resident>,

We really enjoy having you (you and your family) as one of our satisfied homeowners and appreciate the confidence you have shown in our company.
I could use your help.

I would love to be able to talk with some of your friends that might like to live here like you do and discuss with them how they could enjoy living here at <name of your community>.

Please use the enclosed stamped, addressed postcard to jot down the names and contact information for anyone that said they would like to live here or others that you think should see what we're all about.

I'll let you know what I find out and when they plan on visiting. I'll even arrange to bring them by to see you when they visit.

Thanks again for your help.

Let me know if I can do anything for you.

Printed Notecard To An

Established Resident

Rather than a letter, you may choose to use a notecard imprinted with the name and logo of your company or community that you print out on your computer to contact an existing resident that you know. It's less formal than a letter, and it is nice way to ask for referrals.

<First name or names of your resident>,

We really appreciate having you (you and your family) as one of our homeowners (having you call <name of your community or name of the village or neighborhood at your community> home).

I could use your help.

I would love to be able to talk with some of your friends or associates that might like to live here like you do and discuss how they could enjoy life here at <your community>.

I have enclosed a stamped, addressed postcard for you to jot down the names and contact information for anyone that said they would like to live here or others that you think should hear or see what we're all about.

If you prefer, you can email the information to me at <email address> or bring it by the office when you stop in for a cup of coffee.

I'll let you know what I find out when I speak with them and when they plan on visiting. I'll even arrange to bring them by to see you when they visit.

Thanks again for your help.

Let me know if I can do anything for you.

Handwritten Notecard To An Established Resident

Instead of mailing something "typed," you may want to use an informal handwritten notecard to reach out to your established residents and ask them for referrals.

———

<First name or names of your resident>,

We really appreciate having you (you and your family) as one of our homeowners, and I could use your help.

I have enclosed a stamped, addressed postcard for you to jot down the names and contact information for anyone that you think should see what we're all about. If you prefer, you can email the information to me at <email address> or drop it by the office.

Thanks again for your help. Let me know if I can do anything for you.

Email To An Established Resident

Use this less formal email message for a more immediate way to reach out to your established residents and ask for referrals.

———

<First name of your resident>,
We really appreciate having you (you and your family) as one of our homeowners (having you call <name of your community or name of the village or neighborhood at your community> home).

I could use your help.

I would love to be able to talk (meet) with some of your friends that might like to live here like you do and discuss with them how they could enjoy living here at <name of your community>.

Just hit the "reply" button and send along (include, furnish) their names and their contact information for anyone that said they would like to live here or others that you think need to (should) hear (see) what we're all about.

I'll let you know what I find out and when they plan on visiting. I'll arrange to bring them by to see you when they visit.

Thanks again for your help. Let me know if I can do anything for you.

Printed Notecard To A "Lost Sale"

This is one case where a letter is not a good choice because it may appear too formal or not get opened. So choose a notecard imprinted with the name and logo of your company or community that you print out on your computer to contact people who have bought a new home from someone else. This is a good format to use to congratulate them and ask for referrals.

———

<First name or names of your former customer>,

Congratulations and good luck on your new home.

I'm glad I got the opportunity to meet and work with you as you were looking for your new home. Thank you for considering <name of your community or company>.

My company and I wish you many years of enjoyment and happiness in your new home. All the best to you.

If there's anything I can do for you personally, please let me know.

If you know (can think of) anyone who might like the type of homes that we are offering, please let me know.

Again, best wishes in your new home.

Handwritten Notecard To A "Lost Sale"

Instead of mailing something "typed," you may want to use something less formal such as a handwritten notecard to reach out to people who bought a new home from someone else as you congratulate them and ask for referrals.

——————

<First name or names of your former customer>,

Congratulations on your new home and good luck.

Thank you for considering <name of your community or company>. We wish you many years of enjoyment and happiness in your new home. All the best to you.

If there's anything I can do for you personally, please let me know.

If you think of anyone who might like the type of homes that we are offering, please let me know.

Handwritten Greeting Card
Note To A "Lost Sale"

Use this handwritten note as an enclosure or on the inside of a purchased "Congratulations" greeting card to send people who bought a new home from someone else as you congratulate them and ask for referrals.

<First name or names of your former customer>,

Congratulations on your new home.
Thanks for considering <name of your community or company>. All the best to you and many years of enjoyment and happiness in your new home.

If there's anything I can do for you personally, please let me know.

Also, if you think of anyone who might like the type of homes that we are offering, please let me know.

Email To A "Lost Sale"

Use this informal email message for a more immediate way to contact people who bought a new home from someone else as you congratulate them and ask for referrals.

<First name of your former customer>,

Congratulations on your new home and good luck to you.

I'm glad I got the opportunity to meet and work with you as you were looking for your new home.

Thank you for considering <name of your community or company>.

All of us here at <name of your company or community — or both> wish you many years of enjoyment and happiness in your new home. All the best to you (you and your family)!

If there's anything I can do for you personally, please let me know.

If you know or hear of anyone who might like the type of homes that we are offering, please let me know.

As you may recall, we offer <brief statement of type of home or community, such as affordable townhomes, luxury single family homes, low-maintenance coach homes, etc. from {price range}>.

Again, best wishes in your new home.

7

Making It Work

An Entrepreneurial Approach

As a salesperson responsible for your own production and income, you are an entrepreneur. No customers are guaranteed or provided (except those who respond to your marketing and arrive on their own).

Some may come through advertising and marketing, but they don't come in the box that you can purchase at the office supply store.

Each day, you essentially start from scratch. You don't know how many you'll have a chance to talk with or who they will be. Some days there might not be anyone who walks through your front door or otherwise contacts you.

You examine your options for customers — the lifeblood of your business — and determine that you have three viable choices.

Your Three Customer Options

Option one — you stay in your model home or sales center and greet the traffic that walks in, telephones, or emails from traditional marketing sources — principally supplied by your company or builder.

This includes all forms of print advertising in newspapers and magazines (including new homes guides), electronic media (such as radio and TV), internet (your website, social media, and internet advertising), and broker traffic.

Add to that any advertising you do on your own, including direct mail or flyers.

Of course, you maintain post-visit Follow-Through® contact with everyone you meet according to their level of interest and ability to make a decision.

Option two — you reach out to people you don't know or haven't met. You involve strangers in your business and begin building sales and referrals with their help. This is discussed in my companion book for lead generation: **"Making New Friends:** *Connecting With Strangers For More New Home Sales."*

Option three — you talk to people you already know and begin developing your own leads with them. That is what we have been discussing in this book.

It's these second and third options that are going to give you the additional edge and earning power over other new home salespeople in your market.

Most new home salespeople are content to work with the traffic that walks through their front door, and that created through incidental broker traffic and referrals.

This is unpredictable and short-sided. It is not a dependable or consistent form of lead generation.

Empowering Yourself For Success

With the knowledge that you can produce your own leads and make traffic appear that you have generated, you can be an outstanding success.

This is powerful.

Some leads you will generate from people that you haven't met yet. You'll focus on making new connections with strangers and learning which ones you might be able to help and which can lead you to their friends.

However, starting with your circle of contacts and beginning there is very empowering. There is no pressure to meet people before you can start asking for help. Begin with people that you think might be looking for a new home themselves or can introduce you to others.

As long as you don't give the impression that your friendship is conditioned upon them giving you the name of someone to talk with, your friends will still be your friends whether they can help you or not.

Knowledge is power, and in this case it is knowing that you can produce the traffic you need to be successful. This is in addition to what your builder provides through conventional or traditional marketing and advertising — or in place of it.

Begin acting as if the only traffic you're going to get is what you produce for yourself. Then anything your builder supplies is a bonus.

Empowerment Is Taken

By generating your own leads — by reaching out to people that you don't know as well as utilizing your circle of contacts — you're going to be adding an element to your sales program that most builders and new home salespeople are missing.

There is no effective limit to the number of leads that you can generate this way.

This truly can make the difference in your success and enable you to thrive in your marketplace when other builders and new home salespeople are just competing for the same pool of people.

Empowering yourself to begin generating your own leads — by working with friends or strangers — is not something you have to be invited to do or given permission to start.

Empowerment is taken. It is not given.

Just decide that generating your own leads is something that makes sense for you to do — even if you're not totally comfortable with the idea of approaching your family, friends, and acquaintances and talking with them about your business.

However, just doing that will empower you to begin expanding your business and taking responsibility for producing the most crucial element of your sales program — your future customers.

Going Beyond The Obvious

While talking to people that you already know and asking them for referrals will net you many additional opportunities to make sales, other aggressive new home salespeople can do the same thing.

They may not be as comprehensive as you are or able to identify the variety of people you can contact, but starting with referrals from existing satisfied customers and from family and friends are common ways to generate more traffic.

Add to that, the broker network that most new home salespeople try to attract for sales, and you'll soon see that this is quite competitive.

However, when you begin to contact more than just your friends and the top producing brokers that you know — more than just the obvious — you'll be doing what hardly anyone else in your market is doing.

When you reach out to people that you know professionally, ones that you know through the construction of your homes, merchants that you patronize, and even "lost sales," you're going to be finding opportunities that just aren't there for the people who aren't looking for them.

Then, you can also use some of the scenarios that are in my companion lead generation book, *"Making New Friends: Connecting With Strangers To Make More New Home Sales,"* for meeting and working with people you don't know currently.

Reaching out to total strangers and strategically contacting other businesspeople and professionals in your marketplace that can help you in your business are ways that you can be intentional about expanding your business.

Few other builders and new home salespeople in your market will come close to the type of lead generation you'll be capable of producing.

Intentionally Going After Success

Making the decision that you want to have more traffic than you're getting now through traditional sources — and that you want it on a more consistent basis — is the first step to becoming a great traffic generator.

It is a conscious decision, and it requires willpower. No one reaches this intentional decision without the earnest desire to act on it — unless it is just wishful thinking.

Wanting more traffic, like it sure would be nice to have, is entirely different than doing something to actually make it happen.

This works in all market conditions — very active, competitive markets to very stubborn ones.

As long as there are homes to sell and people to buy them, the techniques and strategies of traffic generation that I've discussed will work for you.

You're In Charge Now

The amount of traffic you can produce is limited only by your ambition and the amount of time devoted to it.

You have been given several scenarios in this book. Expand from there. This is a good start, but it is not intended as a comprehensive list.

You have to own your customer base — not in a legal sense but in a responsibility one. You have to continually add to it so it doesn't get stale. Own the creation of additional leads.

Your paradigm needs to be that you're in charge of producing the people that you meet with in your sales center or model home.

Act as if the only traffic you're going to get is what you produce for yourself.

Then anything else that comes your way through traditional marketing or incidental referrals is a bonus.

Not every person you talk to will want to or be able to help you, but as long as you are committed to developing your own leads, you are going to be successful.

You hold the key.

Steve Hoffacker

Steve Hoffacker, CAPS, MCSP, MIRM, is the manager at Hoffacker Associates LLC, a sales training (new home sales, universal design, and aging-in-place) and coaching company based in West Palm Beach, Florida.

Steve is an award-winning, internationally-recognized and experienced new home salesperson and sales trainer, as well as a universal design/aging-in-place safety and accessibility sales trainer and instructor.

For more than 30 years, he has helped homebuilders, new home salespeople, contractors and remodelers, new home marketers, designers, architects, occupational therapists, real estate sales professionals, and others to be more visible, competitive, profitable, and effective — and to really enjoy themselves as they pursue their business and create wonderful customer experiences.

Steve wants you and your company to be successful and has created this and many other books to help make that happen.

This book will be a great resource to help you take your business to another level and outpace the competition.

Use these strategies and concepts for your professional success.